DEFORMITY:

A N

E S S A Y.

By WILLIAM HAY, Efq;

———*Te confule*; *dic tibi quis fis*:
——— *E cælo defcendit* γνωθαι σεαυlον.
Juv. Sat. 11.

THE SECOND EDITION.

L O N D O N:

Printed for R. and J. DODSLEY, in *Pall-mall,*
and Sold by M. COOPER, in *Pater-nofter Row.*
M DCC LIV.
[Price 1s. 6d.

———*Te consule; dic tibi qui sis:*
——— *E cælo descendit* γνωθαι σεαυτον

Trans: Take counsel of yourself and tell yourself what you are:
The maxim "know thyself" comes down from the heavens.

(lines 33 and 27) (Juvenal, "Satire 11," trans. Ramsay, 223).

WILLIAM HAY

Deformity: An Essay

Edited with an introduction by
KATHLEEN JAMES-CAVAN

English Literary Studies
University of Victoria
2004

ENGLISH LITERARY STUDIES
Published at the University of Victoria

Founding Editor
Samuel L. Macey

GENERAL EDITOR
Stephen A. C. Scobie

EDITORIAL BOARD
Thomas R. Cleary
Evelyn M. Cobley
Kathryn Kerby-Fulton
Robert M. Schuler
Lisa A. Surridge

BUSINESS MANAGER
Hedy Thompson

ISBN 0-920604-91-9

The ELS Monograph Series is published in consultation with members of the Department by ENGLISH LITERARY STUDIES, Department of English, University of Victoria, P.O. Box 3070, Victoria, B.C., Canada V8W 3W1. ELS gratefully acknowledges the financial support of the Office of the Vice-President Academic, University of Victoria.

ELS Monograph Series No. 92
© 2004 by Kathleen James-Cavan

Cover illustration: Title page of 2nd edition. Thomson-Gale Microfilm.

Printed on acid-free paper, sewn, and bound by
MORRISS PRINTING COMPANY LTD.
Victoria, British Columbia

CONTENTS

Acknowledgements

I am especially grateful to my colleague Ray Stephanson for first pointing me in the direction of Hay's delightful Essay and to Cassandra Phillips for introducing me to disability studies. In completing the edition, I had help from Richard Harris, University of Saskatchewan; David Adams, Manchester University, and Brycchan Carey, Kingston University. The staff at the University of Saskatchewan Interlibrary loans department has cheerfully accommodated my many requests for obscure materials. The generous assistance provided by the University of Saskatchewan sabbatical fund enabled me to travel to research libraries in the U.K. Stephen Scobie has given valuable advice in helping me prepare the work for publication. For his encouragement, I thank Paul Bidwell, chair of my department. To Peter Sabor of McGill University I owe a debt of gratitude for setting me on this track several years ago. I thank my husband, Stephen Cavan, and our children, Nick, Sophia, and Bryn for their support.

To my parents, Germaine and Terry James.

Introduction

The Deformed Gentleman

Born in 1695 to William and Barbara Hay at Glyndebourne in Sussex, William Hay was orphaned at five and had lost "all the natural protectors of infancy" by the time he was 14 years old.[1] He matriculated at Christ Church, Oxford in 1712 but left in 1715 without taking a degree, removing to the Middle Temple. A self-described hunchback, Hay explains in his *Deformity: An Essay* that his "Back was bent in . . . [his] Mother's Womb" so that as an adult he was "scarce five Feet high" (p. 24, this edition). A bout of small-pox contracted after his arrival in London sometime between 1715 and 1718 left him with impaired vision.[2] In spite of physical difficulties, Hay toured England and Scotland in 1718, recording extensive notes during that "journey of more than a thousand miles," and travelled through France, Germany, and Holland in 1720.[3] Upon his return to Sussex, Hay became an active county magistrate; his name first appears on the surviving fiats in 1727. Married in 1731 to Elizabeth Pelham, daughter of Thomas Pelham of Catsfield, Sussex, a cousin to the Duke of Newcastle, Hay was "returned as M.P. for Seaford at a by-election in January 1734."[5] In addition to launching Hay's long parliamentary career through the duke's interest, the marriage produced three sons and two daughters but no issue succeeded this generation.[6]

Hay's troubled eyesight and physical disabilities were no obstacle to his activities as both Whig politician and man of letters. Stephen Taylor and Clyve Jones record his frenetic committee work: he was "nominated to 302 committees in the 11 sessions between 1734 and 1744."[7] Hay published poetry, pamphlets, and essays both moral and personal throughout his life but his best-known work was *Deformity: An Essay*, first published in 1754 and reprinted in three editions in Hay's lifetime in addition to a Dublin edition. After his death, the *Essay* was reprinted four times in a collection entitled *Fugitive Pieces on Various Subjects*, published by Robert Dodsley, and appeared finally in 1794 in the *Works*.[8]

Before the Essay, Hay's most significant appearance in print was as the author of *Remarks on the Laws relating to the Poor*, 1735 and 1751. Hay's biographer and nephew, the Rev. Francis Tutté, observes in the preface to the *Works* that Hay's "unwearied endeavours to obtain amendment in the laws relating to the poor prove that his heart, as well as his head, was engaged in that business."[9] Hay criticizes the law for obliging "each Parish to maintain its own Poor" with the result that "[e]very Parish is in a State of expensive War with all the rest of the Nation; regards the poor of all other Places as Aliens; and cares not what becomes of them if it can but banish them from its own Society."[10] He proposes to improve the care of the poor by imposing an equal tax rate for poor relief throughout the country, and centralizing relief efforts as well as work houses.

Eulogized by Tutté for his liberal views and unselfish dedication to public service, Hay appears in the biographical sketch as the model English gentleman and *paterfamilias*. According to Tutté, Hay was one of the first to "ornament cornfields with walks and plantations" and he contributed to the development of the Spitalfields silk industry. He was a "wise and affectionate" parent whose care of his sons did not descend to "partial fondness." The daughters are not mentioned. Although Hay's "income was always small for the place which his birth had assigned him in society," Tutté records that guests were treated hospitably and Hay "willingly mixed in company and conversation." Hay's hunchback, however, the subject of his most popular publication, receives only a passing mention, represented as "the pains and inconveniences of a weak bodily frame."[11] Through its refusal to acknowledge Hay's deformity and its insistence on his conformity to a masculine ideal, Tutté's assessment contrasts vividly with Hay's unapologetic self-portrait in the *Essay*, which rejects the culture's equation of bodily deformity and character defect.

Deformity: An Essay[12]

Combining the genres of memoir, literary and cultural critique, and medical testimony, *Deformity: An Essay* offers a unique glimpse into the lived experience of a person with a disability in enlightenment London. Its mix of genres, allusiveness, and variety of rhetorical strategies has prevented critics from fully evaluating its contribution to the literature of disability. Stephen Pender describes the work as the first to challenge the prevailing notion that character and soul could be "accessed and assessed anatomically" but, in his view, the essay goes no further than insisting that "physical anomaly is *not* an indication of spiritual or cognitive deficiency." Lennard Davis criticizes Hay's essay for "reiterating (although humanizing and questioning to a degree) stereotypes about people with disabilities."[13] The *Essay* is far bolder than these critics suggest. In a culture that valued "A charming Body with a lovely Mind"[14] and,

10

in general, judged of one by the other, William Hay contests his liminal position by redefining his alterity as a fortification of an enlightened middle class culture.[15] The narrative exploits deformity as an "interruptive force that confronts cultural truisms"[16] but moves beyond critique to offer the deformed body as a restorative to the body politic. While the *Essay* repudiates deformity as disabling by claiming advantages for "deformed Persons," it also exposes the fallacies that restrict the deformed author, socially and physically. Beginning with Juvenal's injunction to "tell yourself what you are" and ending with a curious politico-medical testimony, the *Essay* insists throughout on the social virtues of the marked, deformed body, thereby resisting the devaluation of the second term that plagues the binary distinction of ability and disability.[17]

Hay's *Essay* appears at a significant turning point in the history of the notion of disability, when science competed with superstition to account for human, physical differences.[18] The tension is evident as early as 1573 in Ambroise Paré's *Des Monstres et prodiges*, whose list of thirteen specific causes of monsters includes the work of both God and demons alongside quasi-scientific explanations: "the narrowness or the smallness of the womb,"[19] "hereditary or accidental illness," and "the indecent posture of the mother, as when, being pregnant, she has sat too long with her legs crossed, or pressed against her womb." Monstrosity in this volume ranges from hip dysplasia to dwarfism to creatures deemed half human and half animal. A 1569 English translation of Pierre Boaistuau's *Histoires prodigieuses* asserts that the deformed person is a monster born "into the world as wel in contempt of nature, as to the perpetual infamie and grief of their parents" as well as a "scourge of the ire of God."[20] Much of Hay's *Essay* is taken up with responding to similarly defamatory notions informing Francis Bacon's 1625 essay "Of Deformity." Although Bacon argues deformity is not a sign from God, he maintains that the deformed person has "a perpetuall Spurre in himselfe, to rescue and deliver himselfe from Scorne."[21] For Bacon, a deformed body necessarily deforms the character as a result of the deformed person's experience in the world. Hay contends that far from exhibiting the anti-social personality traits described by Bacon, the deformed person contributes materially to the physical, moral, and spiritual improvement of society, a state much desired in enlightenment Britain.[22]

Recognized at the time of its publication and by later readers for representing the "infelicities of personal deformity . . . with great pleasantry and chearfulness,"[23] Hay's essay appears to take seriously Samuel Johnson's second definition of "deformity" as "[r]idiculousness" and the "quality of something worthy to be laughed at."[24] Playing on the words "great" and "small," Hay reminds readers that such eminent but short men as "Esop, the Prince of Orange, Marshal Luxemburg, Lord Treasurer Salisbury, Scarron, and Mr. Pope" were all "Members of our Society."[25] Because a person's actions indicate greatness or smallness of character, in Hay's view, the "great" may behave as badly as the uneducated "small" men of society. The essay exemplifies the irony by citing the popularity among all classes of Broughton's Theatre, a boxing club. On April 11, 1750, John Broughton, the owner of the club, was pummelled into permanent blindness by his opponent; the Duke of Cumberland, Broughton's sponsor, who had wagered heavily in his favour, was among the large audience.[26] Granting that a "mangled Carcass is not a pleasing Sight," Hay questions why "the Great Vulgar encourage these Disorders among the Small"(38). Just as the great may be vulgar, the poor or small may also prove great in virtue. Hay contrasts the religious devotion of his "poor, but honest, Neighbours in the Country" with "those, who fare luxuriously on the Fruits of their Labour" but regularly break the fourth commandment (38). Although the essay exploits what Mitchell and Snyder have called the double bind of representation that announces "the question of disability's ambiguous relationship to morality," it refuses to align the non-deformed with either neutrality or normalcy.[27] In a crucial gesture reversing margin and centre, Hay identifies his audience as those "so oddly (I will not say unhappily) distinguished" and hopes that his essay will be "not unentertaining to others," his non-deformed readers.[28] Having re-worked Juvenal's prayer for a sound mind in a healthy body as "*ut fit mens recta in corpore curvo*, for an upright Mind in a crooked one" (40), Hay concludes by reminding readers that Hogarth's recently published *Analysis of Beauty* "proves incontestably, that . . . [beauty] consists in Curve Lines" (46). Henceforth he hopes for his "Fraternity" that "the Ladies will esteem them *Des Beaux Garçons*" (46). The rhetorical strategies of undermining such binaries as "great" and "small," "crooked" and "upright," and associating beauty with curvature combine to fracture the connections between body and character. It is possible to be both morally "upright" and physically "crooked".

Rather than denying that the body mediates identity, then, Hay responds to Bacon's challenges that the deformed are "*void of Naturall Affection*" and "extreme Bold"[29] by demonstrating that his deformed body produces precisely the upright mind so valorized by his culture. In turn, such a connection to public discourse saves the *Essay* from the sentimentalization that often renders private and apolitical the confessional narrative of disability.[30] Hay shows he is a man of cultivated sensibility by first accounting for and then refuting Bacon's statements.[31] Appropriating as a character description a term often used to define a deformed person's body, Hay suggests that if Bacon means by "*Naturall Affection*" "universal Benevolence, . . . a deformed Person must then be a complete Monster."[32] If Bacon refers to "a partial Regard for Individuals" (35), Hay agrees that deformed people are unlikely to suffer this prejudice. Since deformed persons "are seldom Favourites, and commonly most neglected by Parents, Guardians, and Relations," they are not indebted "for much Fondness" so they have little to repay (35). Indeed his deformity has taught him, unlike the able-bodied, to grieve appropriately the "common Accidents of Life" (35). Hay treats the reader to an intimate disclosure of his "Sensations" so that the "Reader may judge, how far I am an Instance of a deformed Person wanting natural Affection" (38). He says he weeps when he reads of "Virtue or Innocence in Distress" (36) or when he meets with an "heroic Saying, Action, or Character" that provides a moral guide. His examples, Christ and the Oxford martyrs, indicate both strong sensibilities and firmly-held Whig views. Appearing little more than digressive, an extended comparison of "Harry IV of France," whose legendary sympathy for Protestants earns him the epithet "Great," with "Lewis XIV," whom Hay characterizes as "little" for his dissipation and religious intolerance, moves the reader from the autobiographical to the historical and dissolves, in approved public sentiments, the deformed body of its author (37). The contemporary reader instantly recognizes the author as a Whig, Protestant Englishman, even if she or he disagrees with the author's version of history. Finally, Hay depicts his response to the spectacle of physical brutality to show he is not without "Naturall Affection." Made uneasy by the inhumane treatment of animals and saddened by human losses in battle, Hay argues that he is most horrified by the inhumanity of prize-fighting matches. He asserts it is not "Choice, but Affectation" that draws crowds of men to these spectacles "to avoid the Imputation of being Cowards: but when they are at so much Pains to avoid the Imputation, it raises a Suspicion that they are so" (38). Vulgarity, then, like sensibility or "Naturall Affection," is evinced in the actions of the individual rather than prescribed by the body or social status.

To counter Bacon's charge that "all *Deformed Persons* are extreme Bold,"[33] Hay draws attention to his body's defective public display as it is circumscribed by the "little Policy" he employs to avoid physical injury and social embarrassment.[34] Although he asserts that the deformed belong in the world, disability also prevents him from being seen where he ought and from participating in society in the manner expected of a man of his status. Afflicted with "unbecoming Bashfulness" (38) and fearing to expose his "Spider-like Shape," Hay cannot perform the requisite gallant service "when Ladies drop a Fan or Glove"; neither can he rise from his seat in public because he cannot regain his balance with ease (28). He is vulnerable in a crowd "where . . . [his] Back is a convenient Lodgement for the Elbow of any tall Person that is near" (28). Therefore, he does not attend "the House of Peers" when the monarch speaks because he would be "squeezed to death there against the Wall" and would see nothing in any case (29). Lacking the strength to serve his country in a military capacity, he represents his service as MP and magistrate as equivalent to that of two exemplary "Great and Tall" men, Richard Onslow (1697-1760), MP for Guildford 1727-60 and brigadier-general, 1742-60, and John West, Lord Delawar (1693-1766; succ. 1723). In accompanying Onslow in a review of his troops, for example, Hay is "humbled" by walking with him among "his tall Men, made still taller by their Caps" (28). Thereafter in the House of Commons he places himself "at some Distance from the General," although the two are "commonly of the same Side of the House" (28). Hay adopts a similar strategy when appearing as a magistrate with Lord Delawar at the quarter sessions: "I always take care to have the Chairman at least between us" (28). Thus, in an action that could be seen as anti-social, he uses physical distance from his acquaintance to avoid feeling "a Worm and no Man" (28). Just as appearing with tall men renders him uncomfortable, so Hay criticizes Steele's satiric Ugly Club[35] for, as it "draws the Eyes of the World too much upon . . . [the deformed]; and theirs too much from the World," the sight of "deformed Persons . . . together . . . doubles the Ridicule."[36] Interpreted through a social code that requires standing for people of importance, attendance on ladies, and appearances with the "Great and Tall," Hay's "Person" is incapable of performing appropriately or with ease. The essay thus exposes the extent to which urban life, especially that of a Member of Parliament, disables the person with a deformity and compromises how his identity is understood.

Although Hay's bodily deformity excludes him from participating in masculine culture, the *Essay* makes no claim for community with other marginalized groups such as women, "the lower Class," and the racialized. Indeed, Hay distances himself from the lower classes whom he depicts as his most frequent abusers. If, as Felicity Nussbaum suggests, the feminine in the eighteenth century is figured as a defective male and the exceptional woman as monstrous,[37] Hay's essay similarly constructs male deformity as effeminizing. He cannot enter into "riotous Assemblies" such as the "Country Fair, Cock-pit, [and] Bear-garden" because he is "liable to Affront, without a power of shewing any Resentment."[38]

He is not "formed for a Masquerade" because "such a Figure would soon be discovered" (26). In this context, his disabled body is his identity. Moreover, he would be exposed to "Abuse from the lower Class" who mix with their "betters" at this entertainment so widely criticized for its promotion of indecency (26). The essay constructs his vulnerability at the masquerade as similar to that of young, unattached females, as represented in the conduct literature of the day.[39] As if to reassert the author's masculinity, however, the text sports two bookends whose gallant and satiric tones are at odds with the rest of the essay. Reflecting the culture's representations of female vanity, the advertisement jokes that

> [t]o promote the Sale of this Piece, Mr. Dodsley was for dedicating it to some reigning Toast: but it was thought more for his Interest to send it into the World, with the Motto inscribed on the Golden Apple adjudged to Venus: for then a thousand Goddesses might seize it as their own.

In addition, all editions after the first end with a "Post-Postscript" in which Hay figures himself as a "Rival" for ladies' lapdogs, a suggestion remarkable for its misogynistic hint of women's sexual deviance.[40] Although these passages stand outside the main body and argument of the text, they emphasize the author's gender and membership in mainstream culture. Hay also favourably compares his experience to that of an African man who offered himself as a candidate in a "venal Borough" that never "took Exception to any man's Character, who came up to their Price; yet they once rejected the best Bidder, because he was a Negroe" (27)[41]. Fortunately, says Hay, his own constituents "never objected to my Person" and he hopes never to give them reason to "object to my Behaviour" (27). While insisting on a disjunction between perceptions of the body and a person's character, this passage reflects the prevalence of the fear of difference that underlies cultural responses to both race and deformity.[42]

Although marked by bodily difference Hay was also a member of the land-owning gentry and shared the class's concern to perpetuate the family name together with the estate through healthy male offspring.[43] Hay's assertion, then, that "Deformity . . . in its Consequences . . . is most commonly an Advantage" (29) directly contradicts the numerous treatises that advised parents, at a time of high infant mortality, how to conceive perfect children and, then, if they had the misfortune to fail, how to correct or at least cover the resulting deformities that would harm a family's genetic line.[44] For Boaistuau, "these monstrous creatures" or people with disabilities such as Hay's hunchback were witnesses "of the incontinence & sinne of the parents."[45] Therefore, he argues, "we must

15

cut of al these generatiõs, which be made against the ordinãce of nature: for by the meanes it often hapneth, that the fruite springing therby is unclean, miserable, monstrous, vicious, odious and destestable, aswel to spirites & devils, as to men & families."[46] In the seventeenth century, Nicolas Andry in his *Orthopaedia: Or, the Art of Correcting and Preventing Deformities in Children*[47] states that care of the body is both a social and religious duty.

> We are born for one another and ought to shun having anything about us that is shocking; and even though a Person should be left alone in the World, he ought not to neglect his body so as to let it become ugly; for this would be contradicting the Intention of the Creator. [48]

In spite of the emphasis on the avoidance of deformity, Andry does not recommend, in the case of the face, making any permanent alterations: "even in Deformity, Nature has observed such exact Symmetry, that we cannot justly find anything to correct in it."[49] Nevertheless, it is the duty of parents to prevent and correct "external Defects" so that their children might have "a streight and agreeable Look."[50] For Hay, however, such a "Look" is neither necessary nor an indication of physical, moral, or spiritual health.

An early proponent of the de-medicalization of disability, Hay asserts throughout the essay that "Deformity is a Protection to a Man's Health and Person" and that he enjoys advantages unavailable to his able-bodied colleagues.[51] In contrast to the advice in the *Orthopaedia*, Hay urges parents not to attempt to correct or hide natural deformities. Through the care taken in his childhood to "correct the Errors of Nature" and "conceal them," Hay learned "to be ashamed of [his] Person" (25) even in adulthood. Arguing "God did not 'make his Works for Man to mend'" (25)[52], Hay naturalizes deformity, asserting "all in me is Nature" (38); that is, his deformed body, of which he is "but Tenant for Life, or (more properly) at Will," is only another example of the range of human variety including "the Deaf, the Dumb, the Lame, and the Blind" (44). In spite of the inconvenience of the mob's special ridicule and the physical restrictions attendant on the hunchback, Hay consoles his "Fraternity" that they are in a "State to be envied" by those with sensory and mobility impairments (44). In addition, the deformed enjoy superiority over the able-bodied. Unlike the "Generality of Mankind [who] . . . wantonly throw away Health (without which Life is not Life)" (30) deformed people are "more careful to preserve Health" especially through temperance, "the great Preservative of Health" (29). Hay sees "many dying before me, who were designed by Nature for a much longer

Life,"[53] while he enjoys good health by refraining from "Wine and all strong Liquors" as well as rich food (30). Moreover, deformity protects against the accidents of the athletic life: "As a deformed Person is not formed for violent Exercise, he is less liable to such Disorders as are the natural Consequence of it" (31). Urging "moderate Exercise . . . which few deformed Persons can want Strength to perform" (30), Hay notes that deformed persons do not engage in dangerous behaviour such as feats of strength or "performing surprising long Journies in a surprising short Time, for no earthly Business, but the Pleasure of relating them" (31). Excluded from the duelling culture, the deformed man is also more pacific than is his able-bodied colleague. Deformity, then, is a civilizing influence that promotes physical health in the deformed individual who, as a devotee of temperance, nurtures "every intellectual Improvement, and . . . every moral Virtue!" (30).

Hay's view that deformity's health benefits are rivalled only by its contributions to the spiritual improvement of society and the individual responds to Bacon's statement that deformed persons, like eunuchs, will use every means at their disposal to "free themselves from Scorne."[54] Hence, Bacon argues, "Kings in Ancient Times, (And at this present in some Countries,) were wont to put Great Trust in Eunuchs . . . as . . . good Spialls, and good Whisperers . . . [rather than] good Magistrates, and Officers."[55] While admitting that deformed persons "can no more be beautiful or strong, than Eunuchs be successful Lovers,"[56] Hay asserts that deformed people have the advantage, through personal experience, of being convinced "of the small Value of most Things which Men value the most" (39). For instance, while Hay's "insuperable Bashfulness" may be "some Obstruction to a Man's Advancement in the World," it is an "Advantage in restraining his Fondness for it" (25). Deformity strengthens the individual's understanding of the transitory nature of worldly things, including the lives of friends and family. Experience teaches deformed persons early in life "not to overvalue what we must soon part with" and that "to be so fond of others, as not to be able to bear their Absence, or to survive them, is . . . but a childish and womanish Weakness" (35). While Bacon ascribes to envy the motives of deformed people and eunuchs, Hay says he has extinguished it, but he admits that the deformed, more than others, may suffer the effects of jealousy. Deformed people are sensible of being "less amiable" because of their lack of beauty and strength and, therefore, suspect they are "less beloved" (39). In this sole instance, Hay allows that bodily deformity results in a character defect; however, because his wife's "Virtues are an Honour to her Family, and her Sex," he draws his example only from his younger days "when Ladies have been more liberal of their Smiles to those, whom I thought in every respect, but Person, my Inferiors" (40). Aware that "if Beauty adds Grace to Virtue it self, vice must be doubly hideous in Deformity," the deformed person has a stronger motive for self-improvement than does an able-bodied person (40). The ambitious deformed person must obtain by hard work "that Regard, which is paid to Beauty at first sight," so that people "no sooner find . . . [the deformed] better than they expected, than they believe them better than they are" (32). In the "beautiful Person, . . . [people] sometimes find themselves imposed upon, and are angry that they have worshipped only a painted idol" (32). A deformed person, therefore, rarely disappoints.

Informed by more than thirty sources, the *Essay* testifies to Hay's claim that one of the greatest advantages to deformity is its tendency to "the Improvement of the Mind," for those of the privileged classes (42). Drawing heavily on Juvenal's tenth satire, the essay includes references to eight other Latin sources, both literary and historical, in addition to essays by Bacon, Montaigne, Fontenelle, and Steele. Hay cites the work of French and English historians of the late seventeenth and early eighteenth centuries as well as poetry and drama from Milton to Pope. As three of his sources, those by Jonas Hanway, William Hogarth, and William Melmoth, were published only months before *Deformity: An Essay*, Hay shows that he is also well-informed about contemporary literature. As wit[57] is vital to the deformed person in overcoming the "Ridicule and Contempt [that] are a certain consequence of Deformity," (40) the pursuit of such an education is the "proper Province" of the deformed person (31). Hay's class bias, however, prevents him from recognizing adequately deformity's effects on the "lower Class." Although he acknowledges that a deformed man cannot work as a soldier, sailor, chairman or porter, he proposes substitute employments open only to those with access to education and influence: schoolmaster, playwright, or "Merchant on the Exchange" (31). Setting these problems aside, Hay asserts that "[a] Man, that cannot shine in his Person, will have recourse to his Understanding" (42). Such a man — Hay consistently ignores the position of deformed women — will naturally pursue lasting fame through virtue and wisdom in imitation of Socrates' example, rather than through amassing fortunes or building monuments, both liable to decay. Moreover, since deformity places him "more out of Danger, than even Virtue could" through exclusion from the economy of sexual desire (whether of men, women, or self), Hay argues that he is well placed, through his efforts at self-improvement, to provide service "owing to" rather than in spite of deformity (42). Hay argues that deformity "at least should be a Restraint on my Conduct, lest my Conduct make me more deformed" (43). Although the argument perpetuates the long history of the asexuality of the disabled, it nevertheless provides a forceful counter example to the culture's association of bodily deformity with character defects.

Having begun with the aim of writing "of Deformity with Beauty; and by a finished Piece to attone [sic] for an ill-turned Person" (24), Hay concludes by repudiating the very categories of beauty and deformity that have been so consistently revalued throughout. In rupturing the culture's connection between deformity and character defects such as excessive boldness and deviousness, the essay argues forcefully, if somewhat contradictorily, for the character advantages and health benefits available to the deformed issuing from the body. The essay's conclusion, then, a curious testimonial entitled "My Case," appears to overturn this thesis by outlining the details of his struggle with bladder stones. Admitting that his temperate practice of drinking "raw water" has caused him to suffer from the stone for several years,[58] Hay claims he has found ease and comfort by taking "Mrs. *Stephens*'s Medicine in the solid Form, three Ounces a Day, for about five Years" (45). After describing his "Regimen" and its "Effects," he concludes the medicine is lithontriptic, lenitive, and preventive of the stone. On the surface, this admission of ill health alongside a strong, commercial endorsement appears to defeat the essay's central argument. By specifically mentioning Joanna Stephens's medicine and naming its beneficial properties, however, Hay aligns himself with a host of scientists and worthies, including the Prime Minister and the Speaker of the House of Commons, who also publicly supported the medication when its recipe was purchased by Parliament in 1740.[59] Thus, this consequence of deformity and resulting temperance, while barring Hay from "the Field of false Honour," nevertheless allows him to take an active part in the more modern, masculine pursuit of scientific truth. In addition, since all bodies rot and "lying Marble will decay," Hay literally provides himself "a Monument" (44) by bequeathing the stone he is sure will be found in his bladder upon his death as an artefact to be "preserved among Sir *Hans Sloane*'s Collections" (44). In the end, Hay's memorial is a fragment of a body, detached from positive or negative value. As the hunchbacked surface of his body disappears from the text along with its transitory representations of beauty and deformity, his bladder stone, together with its medical narrative, remains to benefit human kind. Although the body has dissolved, its internal product, a proof of the consequence of bodily difference, commemorates both Hay and the meanings of deformity among the beauties of the future British Museum.

A Note on the Text

This edition is based on the second edition of *Deformity: An Essay* published by Robert Dodsley in 1754. Changes to this edition, notably the addition of the "Post-postscript" repeated in subsequent editions, suggest that the author saw the second edition through the press. The third edition is a reprint of the second and the "fourth" edition is a Dublin reprint by George Faulkner of the first edition. I have modernized the long "s" but retained Hay's eighteenth-century spellings such as "sate," "attone," "peculier," "journies," and "counterballanced." I have silently corrected errors in the transcription of the Latin quotations while corrections of obvious typographical errors in the English text are noted.

Chronology for William Hay

1695	born August 21 to William and Barbara Hay at Glyndebourne, Sussex
1697	death of father
1697	November 16, mother marries Merrick Jenkins
1699	April, birth of step-brother Charles
1700	death of mother
1701	death of his guardian, maternal grandfather, Sir John Stapeley
1705	sent to school in Newick, 7 miles from Lewes
1709	death of grandmother, Mary Stapeley; Mary Dobell, Hay's maternal aunt, becomes his guardian
1710	attends grammar school at Lewes
1712	March 20, matriculation at Christ Church, Oxford
1715	enters Middle Temple
1715-18	contracts small-pox
1718	tour of England and Scotland
1720	travels to France, Germany, Holland
1723	takes oaths in the court of King's Bench
1727	becomes justice of the peace in eastern division of Sussex
1728	publishes, anonymously, *Essay on Civil Government*
1730	publishes *Mount Caburn, a poem*
1731	marries Elizabeth Pelham, second daughter of Thomas Pelham, Esq. of Catsfield, Sussex
1732	publishes pamphlet defending the reimposition of the salt tax
1733	July 3, birth of son Thomas
1734	elected M.P. for Seaford
1735	publishes *Remarks on the Laws relating to the Poor, with Proposals for their better Relief and Employment*
1735	June 21, birth of son William
1736	June 27, birth of son Henry
1738-47	commissioner of the Victualling office

1747-54	granted secret service pension of £500 p.a.
1751	publishes second and enlarged edition of *Remarks on the Laws*
1753	publishes *Religio Philosophi*
1754	appointed Keeper of the Records in the Tower
1754	publishes *Deformity: An Essay* and *The Immortality of the Soul. A Poem. Translated from the Latin of Isaac Hawkins Browne, Esq; by William Hay, Esq.*
1754	October, death of son Henry
1755	publishes *Translations and Imitations of Select Epigrams of Martial*
1755	dies June 22

****

ADVERTISEMENT.

To promote the Sale of this Piece, Mr. Dodsley was for dedicating it to some reigning Toast: but it was thought more for his Interest to send it into the World, with the Motto inscribed on the Golden Apple adjudged to *Venus*: for then a thousand Goddesses might seize it as their own.

****

Dedication.
Detur Pulchriori.
To The
Greatest Beauty[1]

****

DEFORMITY; AN Essay, &c.

It is offensive for a Man to speak much of himself: and few can do it with so good a Grace as *Montaigne*[2]. I wish I could; or that I could be half so entertaining or instructive.[3] My Subject however will be my Apology: and I am sure it will draw no Envy upon me. Bodily Deformity is visible to every Eye; but the Effects of it are known to very few; intimately known to none but those, who feel them; and they generally are not inclined to reveal them. As therefore I am furnished with the necessary Materials, I will treat this uncommon Subject at large: and to view it in a philosophical Light is a Speculation which may be useful to Persons so oddly (I will not say unhappily) distinguished; and perhaps not unentertaining to others.

I do not pretend to be so ingenious as *Montaigne*, but it is in my power to be as ingenuous. I may with the same *Naïveté*[4] remove the Veil from my mental as well as personal Imperfections; and expose them naked to the World. And when I have thus anatomized[5] my self, I hope my Heart will be found sound and untainted, and my Intentions honest and sincere.[6]

Longinus[7] says, that *Cecilius* wrote of the Sublime in a low Way: on the contrary, Mr. Pope calls *Longinus* "The great Sublime he draws."[8] Let it be my Ambition to imitate *Longinus* in Style and Sentiment: and like *Cecilius*, to make these appear a Contrast to my Subject: to write of Deformity with Beauty: and by a finished Piece to attone for an ill-turned Person.

If any Reader imagines, that a Print[9] of me in the Frontispiece of this Work would give him a clearer Idea of the Subject; I have no Objection; provided he will be at the Expence of ingraving. But for want of it let him know; that I am scarce five Feet high: that my Back was bent in my Mother's Womb:[10] and that in Person I resemble *Esop*, the Prince of *Orange*, Marshal *Luxemburg*, Lord Treasurer *Salisbury, Scarron*, and Mr. *Pope*:[11] not to mention *Thersites* and *Richard* the Third; whom I do not claim as Members of our Society:[12] the first being a Child of the Poet's Fancy; the last misrepresented by Historians, who thought they must

24

draw the Devil in a bad Shape. But I will not (on this Occasion) accept of *Richard's* Statue from the Hand of any Historian, or even of *Shakespear* himself; but only from that of his own Biographer,[13] who tells us (and he ought to know) that *Richard* was a handsome Man.

As I have the greatest Reason to thank God, that I was born in this Island, and enjoy the Blessings of this Majesty's Reign; let me not be unthankful, that I was not born in *Sparta!* where I had no sooner seen the Light, but I should have been deprived of it; and have been thrown as a useless thing,[14] into a Cavern by Mount *Taygetus!* Inhuman *Lycurgus!* thus to destroy your own Species! Surrounded by the Innocents, whom you have murdered, may I not haunt you among the Shades below for this Barbarity? That it was ill Policy, the glorious List of Names, which I have produced, is a Proof: your own *Agesilaus*,[15] confutes your Maxim: and I hope to confute it too by my own Behaviour. Is the Carcass the better part of the Man? And is it to be valued by Weight, like that of Cattle in a Market?

Instead of this *Lacedemonian* Severity, those, who had the Care of my Infancy, fell into another Extreme; and, out of Tenderness, tried every Art to correct the Errors of Nature; but in vain: for (as I think it is Mr. *Dryden* says)

'God did not make his Works for Man to mend.'[16]

When they could not do that, they endeavoured to conceal them: and taught me to be ashamed of my person, instead of arming me with true Fortitude to despise any Ridicule or Contempt of it. This has caused me much Uneasiness in my younger Days: and it required many Years to conquer this Weakness. Of which I hope now there are but little Remains left. This ill Management gave me too an insuperable Bashfulness: and although I have passed the Course of my whole Life among the Better Part of Mankind; I have always felt a Reluctance to produce a bad Figure: which may be some Obstruction to a Man's Advancement in the World: but an Advantage in restraining his Fondness for it.

Unmerited Reflections on a Man's Person are hard of Digestion. Men of Understanding have felt them. Even Mr. *Pope* was not invulnerable in this Part. For when the Dunces were foiled by his Writings, they printed a Caricatura of his Figure: and it is evident that this stung him more than a better Answer: for he ranks it among the most atrocious Injuries.[17] I never in my Life received the least Affront on this Head from any Gentleman I ever conversed with; or from any one, who had the least Pretension to that Name: for I should be a Churl indeed, if I esteemed as such any little innocent Pleasantry of a Friend, which is rather an

Instance of sincere Kindness and Affection: and I should be unfit to sit at Table with him, should I resent his Congratulations on my emerging from an Eclipse of a Sirloin of Roastbeef, or of a Bowl of Punch, that stood between us. But the Scene changes extremely when I get into a Mob; where Insolence grows in Proportion, as the man sinks in Condition: and where I can scarce pass without hearing some Affront. But I am now unmoved with that Scurrility, which used to affect me when I was young. Their Title of Lord I never much valued; and now I entirely despise: and yet they will force it upon me as an Honour, which they have a Right to bestow, and which I have none to refuse. This Abuse is grown into such a Habit with the Rabble, that an *Irish* Chairman often uses it, when he asks me to take a Chair;[18] and sometimes a Beggar, when he demands an Alms.

This Difference of Behaviour towards me hath given me the strongest Idea of the Force of Education; and taught me to set a right Value upon it. It is certainly the Stamp of a Man's Character: it distinguishes the base from the valuable Metal: and is the Barrier between the Mob and the civilized Part of Mankind. This Usage hath also been a great Advantage to me: for it hath made me (like *Horace*)[19] fly from the Vulgar to the Company and Conversation of my Superiors, where I am sure to be easy. I have ever enjoyed it; and though I want polite Qualities to recommend me, I cannot say, I was ever ill received by them. Moreover, these Abuses from my Inferiors often furnish me with generous Reflections. I sometimes recollect the Expression of *Brutus* in *Shakespear*, "Your *Words* pass by me as the idle Wind, which I regard not:"[20] at other Times a Saying (I think) of *Socrates*; "Shall I be angry if an Ass kick at me? It is his Nature so to do."[21] But personal Reflections of this kind are almost unknown among Persons of high Rank. It must therefore be only a *French* Romance, that gave rise to the Report, that our great and glorious Deliverer[22] once called *Luxemburg* crooked-back Fellow: who replied, that he *could* not know that he was so, for he had never seen his Back.

When by some uncommon Accident I have been drawn into a Country Fair, Cock-pit, Bear-garden, or the like riotous Assemblies, after I have got from them, I have felt the Pleasure of one escaped from the Danger of a Wreck: for all the Time I am present, I consider my self as liable to Affront, without a Power of shewing any Resentment; which would expose me to ten-fold Ridicule. Nor am I formed for a Masquerade; where such a Figure would soon be discovered; nor escape Abuse from the lower Class, whom the Mask introduces to their Betters; and where all indulge a greater Liberty of Behaviour.

I always had an Aversion in my Childhood to Dancing-masters: and studied all Evasions to avoid their Lessons; when they were forced upon me: for I was ever conscious to my self, what an untoward Subject they had to work on. I carried this a little too far; and have sometimes wished I had sacrificed a little more to the Graces. The Neglect of this has left behind it an Awkwardness in some Part of my outward Gesture and Behaviour: and I am sensible, that I might by Care and Habit have corrected some Things now grown inveterate; and that from a natural Dislike to Trifles I neglected some Forms too much.

Bodily Deformity is very rare: and therefore a Person so distinguished must naturally think, that he has had ill Luck in a Lottery, where there are above a thousand Prizes to one Blank. Among 558 Gentlemen in the House of Commons I am the only one that is so. Thanks to my worthy Constituents, who never objected to my Person; and I hope never to give them cause to object to my Behaviour. They are not like a venal Borough, of which there goes a Story; that, though they never took Exceptions to any Man's Character, who came up to their Price; yet they once rejected the best bidder, because he was a Negroe.[23]

I never was, nor ever will be, a member of the Ugly Club[24] and I would advise those Gentlemen to meet no more: For though they may be a very ingenious and facetious Society; yet it draws the Eyes of the World too much upon them, and theirs too much from the World. For who would choose to be always looking at bad Pictures, when there is so great a Collection to be met with of good ones, especially among the Fair Sex: who, if they will not admit them to be Intimates, will permit them to be distant Admirers. When deformed Persons appear together, it doubles the Ridicule, because of the Similitude; as it does, when they are seen with very large Persons, because of the Contrast. Let them therefore call *Minerva* to their Aid in both Cases.

There are many Great and Tall Men, with whom I shall always esteem it an Honour to converse: and though their Eyes are placed in a much higher Parallel, they take care never to overlook me: and are always concerned, if by Chance they happen to strike[25] my Hat with the Elbow. When standing or walking, we indeed find some Difficulty in the Conversation; for they are obliged to stoop down, as in search of a Pin, while I am looking up, as if taking the Height of a Star with a Quadrant. And I own I sometimes use a little Policy, that the Contrast may not be too remarkable.

General *O*.[26] is Brother in Blood and in Worth to one of the greatest and best Men of the Age: and a brave Spirit is lodged in a large Person. The Man, who stood intrepid by his Majesty's Side in the glorious Day of *Dettingen*,[27] and afterwards by that of his Royal Highness in the more unfortunate one of *Fontenay*,[28] is now placed at the Head of a Troop of Horse Grenadiers, to guard that Prince, whom he hath so long and faithfully served. I have the Honour to be well known to him: and I once accidentally accompanied him to see the Horses of his Troop. I never was more humbled, than when I walked with him among his tall Men, made still taller by their Caps. I seemed to myself a Worm and no Man: and could not but inwardly grieve, that when I had the same Inclination to the Service of my Country and Prince, I wanted their Strength to perform it. — As a Member of the House of Commons, I sometimes use the Precaution to place my self at some Distance from the General, though I am commonly of the same Side of the House.[29]

Lord *D.*[30] is another brave Officer at the head of one of his Majesty's Troops of Guards; and one of the tallest of his Subjects: an ancient Peer: an able Senator: and (what is much to the Honour of any Peer) an useful Magistrate in the Country. I am always proud of meeting his Lordship at the Quarter Sessions:[31] but I always take care to have the Chairman at least between us on the Bench; that it may not be too visible to the Country, what a prodigious Disparity there is in every Respect between us.

But I will now divide my Text, in order to discuss it more thoroughly: and will consider the natural Consequences of Bodily Deformity; first, how it affects the outward Circumstances, and lastly, what Turn it gives to the Mind.

It is certain, that the Human Frame, being warped and disproportioned, is lessened in Strength and Activity; and rendered less fit for its Functions. *Scarron* had invented an Engine to take off his hat;[32] and I wish I could invent one to buckle my Shoe, or to take up a thing from the Ground, which I can scarce do without kneeling; for I can bend my Body no farther than it is bent by Nature. For this Reason, when Ladies drop a Fan or Glove, I am not the first to take them up: and often restrain my inclination to perform those little Services, rather than expose my Spider-like Shape. And I hope it will not be construed as Pride, if I do not always rise from my Seat when I ought: for if it is low, I find some Trouble in it; and my Center of Gravity is so ill placed, that I am often like to fall back. Things, hanging within the Reach of others, are out of mine. And what they can execute with Ease, I want Strength to perform. I am in Danger of being trampled on, or stifled, in a Crowd; where my Back is a convenient Lodgment for the Elbow of any tall Person that is near. I can see nothing; and my whole Employment is to guard my Person. I have forborne to attend his majesty in the House of Peers, since I was like to be squeezed to death there against the Wall. I would willingly come thither when his Majesty commands, but he is too gracious to expect Impossibilities. Besides, when I get in, I can never have the Pleasure of seeing on the Throne, one of the best Princes, who ever sate on it. These and many others are the Inconveniences continually attending a Figure like mine. They may appear grievous to Persons not used to them; but they grow easier by Habit: and though they may a little disturb, they are not sufficient to destroy the Happiness of Life; of which, at an Average, I have enjoyed as great a Share as most Men. And perhaps one Proof of it may be my writing this Essay: not intended as a Complaint against Providence for my Lot, but as an innocent Amusement to my self and others.

I cannot tell what Effect Deformity may have on the health: but it is natural to imagine, that as the inward Parts of the Body must in some measure comply with the outward Mould; the Form of the latter being irregular, the first cannot be so well placed and disposed to perform their Functions: and that generally deformed Persons would not be healthy or long-lived. But this is a Question best determined by Facts: and in this Case the Instances are too few, or unobserved, to draw a general Conclusion from them. And Health is, more than is commonly thought, in a Man's own Power; and the Reward of Temperance, more than the Effect of Constitution: which makes it still more difficult to pass a Judgment. *Esop* could not be young when he died: and might have lived longer, if he had not been murdered at *Delphos*.[33] The Prince of *Orange* scarce passed the Meridian of Life: and the Duke of *Luxemburgh* died about the Age of sixty-seven.[34] The Lord Treasurer *Burleigh* (the Honour of whose Company I claim on the Authority of *Osborn*)[35] lived to seventy-eight: but his Son the Earl of Salisbury, who died about fifteen Years after him, could not reach near that Age. I have heard (but know not if it is true) that Mr. *Pope*'s Father was deformed, and he lived to be seventy-five: whereas the Son died in middle Age; if he may be said to die, whose Works are immortal.[36] My Father was not deformed, but active, and my Mother a celebrated Beauty; and I am so unlike them, have lived to a greater Age: and daily see my Acquaintance, of a stronger Frame, quitting the Stage before me.[37]

But I leave it to better Naturalists to determine, whether Deformity, abstractedly considered, is prejudicial to Health; for in its Consequences, I believe, it is most commonly an Advantage. Deformed Persons have a less Share of Strength than others, and therefore should naturally be more careful to preserve it: and as Temperance is the great Preservative of Health, it may incline them to be more temperate. I have Reason to think that my own weak Frame and Constitution have prolonged my Life to this present Date. But I should impose upon my Reader, and affront heaven, if I ascribed that to Virtue, which took its Rise from Necessity. Being of a consumptive Disposition, I was alarmed, when young, with frequent spitting of Blood: this made me abstain from Wine and all strong Liquors; which I have now done for near thirty Years. But

(*Incidit in Scyllam cupiens vitare Carybden.*)[38]

By this I fell into another Misfortune; and the Stone was the Consequence of my drinking raw Water: but Care and Perseverance with Abstinence, have so far subdued that Distemper; that at present it is but little Interruption to my Ease or Happiness. And weak as I am, I daily see many dying before me, who were designed by Nature for a much longer Life. And I cannot but lament, that the Generality of Mankind so wantonly throw away Health (without which Life is not Life)[39] when it is so much in their own Power to preserve it. If every Virtue in its Consequence is its own Reward; Temperance is eminently so; and every one immediately feels its good Effect. And I am persuaded that many might arrive at *Cornaro*'s Age, if they did but follow his Example.[40] On thinking upon this Subject, I have adopted many Maxims, which to the World will seem Paradoxes; as certain true Geographical Theorems do to those, who are unacquainted with the Globe. I hold as Articles of Faith (but which may be condemned as Heresies in many a General Council assembled about a large Table) That the smallest Liquors are best.[41] That there never was a good Bowl of Punch; nor a good Bottle of Champaign, Burgundy, or Claret. That the best Dinner is one Dish. That an Entertainment grows worse in proportion as the Number of Dishes increase. That a Fast is better than a Lord Mayor's Feast. That no Conoisseur ever understood good Eating. That no Minister of State or Ambassador ever gave a good Entertainment. No King ever sate down to a good Table. And that the Peasant fares better than the Prince, &c. &c. &c. Being inspired with such Sentiments, what Wonder is it, if I sometimes break out into such Ejaculations. O Temperance! Thou Goddess most worthy to be adored! Thou Patroness of Health! Thou Protector of Beauty! Thou Prolonger of Life! Thou Insurer of Pleasure! Thou Promoter of Business! Thou Guardian of the Person! Thou Preserver of the Understanding! Thou Parent of every intellectual Improvement, and of every moral Virtue!

Another great Preservative of Health is moderate Exercise; which few deformed Persons can want Strength to perform. I never chose long Journies, and they have been fatiguing to me; but I never found my self worse for Fatigue. And (before I was troubled with the Stone) I have on occasion rid fifty Miles in a Day; or walked near twenty. And, though now slow in my Motions, I can be on my Feet the greatest part of the Day; and cannot be said to lead a sedentary Life. As a deformed Person is not formed for violent Exercise, he is less liable to such Disorders as are the natural Consequence of it. He will also escape many Accidents, to which men of athletic Make, and who glory in their Strength, are always exposing themselves to make Trial and Proof of it. If he cannot carry an Ox, like *Milo*; he will not, like *Milo*, be hand-cuffed in the Oak, by attempting to rend it.[42] He will not be the Man, that shall ride from *London* to *York* in a Day, or to *Windsor* in an Hour for a Wager; or that shall be perpetually performing surprising long Journies in a surprising short Time for no earthly Business, but the Pleasure of relating them. Conscious of his own Weakness, he will be cautious of running into Places or Occasions of Danger. I deny my self some Entertainments, rather than venture into a Crowd, knowing how unequal I am to a Struggle in it: and if any sudden Quarrel should arise, how ill I am qualified for such an Encounter. One Blow from a *Slack* or a *Broughton* would infallibly consign me over to *Charon*.[43] Nature too calls on deformed Persons to be careful not to offer such Affronts, as may call them forth into the Field of false Honour, where they cannot acquit themselves well for want of Strength and Agility: and they are securer from such Affronts themselves; since others will consider the little Credit they will gain, by compelling them to appear on that Scene.[44] On the whole I conclude, that Deformity is a Protection to a Man's Health and Person; which (strange as it may appear) are better defended by Feebleness than Strength.

Let me now consider the Influence of Bodily Deformity on a Man's Fortune. Among the lower Class, he is cut off from many Professions and Employments. He cannot be a Soldier, he is under Standard: he cannot be a Sailor, he wants Activity to climb the Rigging: he cannot be a Chairman or Porter, he wants Strength to bear the Burthen. In higher Life, he is ill qualified for a Lawyer, he can scarce be seen over the Bar:[45] for a Divine; he may drop from his Hassock out of Sight in his Pulpit. The Improvement of the Mind is his proper Province: and his Business only such as depends on Ingenuity. If he cannot be a Dancing-master to adjust the Heels; he may be a School-master to instruct the Head. He cannot be a graceful Actor on the Stage; but he may produce a good Play. He would appear ill as a Herald in a Procession; but may pass as a Merchant on the Exchange. He cannot undergo the Fatigue of the Campaign; but he may advise the Operations of it. He is designed by Nature, rather to sleep on *Parnassus*, than to descend on the Plains of *Elis*. He cannot be crowned at the *Olympic Games*; but may be the *Pindar* to celebrate them.[46] He can acquire no Glory by the Sword; but he may by the Pen: and may grow famous by only relating those Exploits, which are beyond his Power to imitate.

Lord *Bacon* (that extensive and penetrating Genius, who pointed out every Part of Nature for Examination) in his Essay on Deformity says, "that, in their Superiors, it quencheth Jealousy towards them, as Persons, that they think they may at pleasure despise: and it layeth their Competitors and Emulators asleep; as never believing they should be in a Possibility of Advancement, till they see them in Possession." But it is much to be doubted, whether this is not more than counterballanced by the Contempt of the World, which it requires no mean Parts to conquer. For if (as I have somewhere read) a good Person is a Letter of Recommendation, Deformity must be an obstruction in the Way to Favour.[47] In this respect therefore deformed Persons set out in the World to a Disadvantage, and they must first surmount the Prejudices of Mankind, before they can be upon a Par with others. And must obtain by a Course of Behaviour that Regard, which is paid to Beauty at first sight. When this Point is once gained, the Tables are turned; and then the Game goes in their Favour: for others sensible of their first Injustice to them, no sooner find them better than they expected, than they believe them better than they are: whereas in the beautiful Person, they sometimes find themselves imposed upon, and are angry that they have worshipped only a painted Idol. For (again Lord *Bacon*'s Words) "neither is it almost seen, that very beautiful Persons are otherwise of great Virtue: they prove accomplished, but not of great Spirit; and study rather Behaviour than Virtue.[48] Whereas deformed Persons, if they be of Spirit, will free themselves from scorn, which must be either by Virtue or Malice; and therefore let it not be marvelled, if they sometimes prove excellent Persons, as was *Agesilaus, Zanger* the Son of *Solomon, Esop, Gasca* President of *Peru*;[49] and *Socrates* may likewise go amongst them, with others." Nay, he says, "in a great Wit Deformity is an Advantage to Rising." [50] And, in another Part of his Works, "they, who by Accident have some inevitable and indelible Mark on their Persons or Fortunes, as deformed Persons, Bastards, &c. if they want not Virtue, generally prove fortunate." [51]

Osborn in his *Historical Memoirs of Queen Elizabeth* informs us; that "she chose the goodliest Persons for her Household Servants; but in her counsellors did not put by Sufficiency, tho' accompanied with a crooked Person; as it chanced in a Father and a Son of the *Cecils*, both incomparable for Prudence."[52] It is well known, the Queen would make the Father (*Burleigh*) sit in her Presence; telling him, that she did not use him for his Legs, but Head. But the Son (afterwards Lord Treasurer and

Earl of *Salisbury*) was not so civilly treated by the Populace; and is an Instance, not only that Envy pursues a great Man, but that the highest Post cannot redeem a deformed one from Contempt; it attends him like his Shadow, and like that too is ever reminding him of his ill Figure; which is often objected for want of real Crimes. For the same Writer says of the same great Man; "that the Misfortunes accompanying him from his Birth did not a little add to that Cloud of Detraction, that fell upon all that he said or did: a Mulct in Nature, like an Optick Spectacle, multiplying much in the sight of the People the Apparitions of Ill."[53] Nor was this Contempt buried with him: it trampled on his Ashes, and insulted his Grave; as appears by an Epitaph, which *Osborn* cites, as void of Wit, as it is full of Scurrility: in one Line of which there is an Epithet, not so elegant, as descriptive of his Person, *viz.* "Little *Bossive* Robin, that was so great."[54]

Such Contempt in general, joined with the Ridicule of the Vulgar, is another certain Consequence of bodily Deformity. For Men naturally despise what appears less beautiful or useful: and their Pride is gratified, when they see such Foils to their own Persons. It is this Sense of Superiority, which is testified by Laughter in the lower sort: while their Betters, who know how little any Man whatsoever hath to boast of, are restrained by good Sense and good Breeding from such an Insult. But it is not easy to say why one Species of Deformity should be more ridiculous than another, or why the Mob should be more merry with a crooked Man, than one that is deaf, lame, squinting, or purblind. Or why should they back-bite me (if I may use the Expression) to my Face, and not laugh at my Face itself for being harrowed by the Small Pox. It is a Back in Alto Relievo that bears all the Ridicule; though one would think a prominent Belly a more reasonable Object of it; since the last is generally the Effect of Intemperance, and of a Man's own Creation. *Socrates* was ugly, but not contemned; and *Philopœmen*[55] of very mean appearance, and though contemned on that Account, not ridiculed; for *Montaigne* says, "Ill Features are but a superficial Ugliness and of little Certainty in the Opinion of Men: but a Deformity of Limbs is more substantial, and strikes deeper in."[56] As it is more uncommon, it is more remarkable: and that perhaps is the true reason, why it is more ridiculed by the Vulgar.

Since this is the Case; I appeal to my Fraternity, whether it is not sound Policy to use Stratagem to guard against their Attacks as much as[57] may be; and since they are deceived by outward Appearances, to call in the Aid of the Taylor, to present them with better Shapes than Nature has bestowed. Against so unfair an Adversary such Fraud is justifiable; tho' I do not approve of it in general. When I was a Child, I was drawn like a Cupid, with a Bow and Arrow in my Hands, and a Quiver on my Shoulder: I afterwards thought this an Abuse, which ought to be corrected: and when I sate for my Picture some Years ago, I insisted on being drawn as I am, and that the strong Marks of the Small Pox might appear in my Face: for I did not choose to colour over a Lye. The Painter said, he never was allowed such Liberty before; and advised him, if he hoped to be in Vogue never to assume it again: for Flatterers succeed best in the World; and of all Flatterers, Painters are the least liable to be detected by those they flatter. Nor are the Ladies the only Persons concerned for their Looks. "*Alexander*[58] chose to have his Picture drawn by *Apelles*, and his Statue formed by *Lysippus*. And the *Spartan Agesilaus* (conscious of his ill Figure) would never suffer any Picture or Statue of him to be taken. He was one of the most considerable Persons of his Age both for civil and military Virtues, insomuch that he justly acquired the Apellation of *Agesilaus* the Great. But tho' Nature had been uncommonly liberal to him in the nobler Endowments of the Mind, she had treated him very unfavourably in those of the Body. He was remarkably low of Stature: had one Leg shorter than the other; and so very despicable a Countenance, that he never failed of raising Contempt in those, who were unacquainted with his moral and intellectual Excellencies. It is no wonder therefore, that he was unwilling to be delivered down to Posterity under the Disadvantages of so unpromising a Figure." I have given the Words of a late very elegant Translation of *Cicero*'s Letters.[59] — On the whole, I could wish, that Mankind would be more candid and friendly with us; and instead of ridiculing a distorted Person, would rally the Irregularities of the Mind: which generally are as visible as those of the Person; but being more common, they pass with little Notice as well in high as low Life. Mæcenas would laugh at any Irregularity in *Horace*'s Dress,[60] but not at any Caprice in his Behaviour, because it was common and fashionable: so a Man's Person, which is the Dress of his Soul, only is ridiculed, while the vicious Qualities of it escape. — Let me add, that if ridiculing another's Person is in no Case to be justified, the ill Treatment of it must be highly criminal: what then must we think of *Balbus*, a *Roman* Quæstor in *Spain*, who wantonly exposed to wild Beasts a certain noted Auctioneer at Seville for no other reason, but because he was deformed. This is related in a Letter to Cicero by Asinius Pollio, the most accomplished Gentleman of that Age; who calls Balbus a Monster for this and other acts of Barbarity.[61] I am glad he has preserved the memory of this poor Man; whom I here consecrate to Fame; and place foremost in the glorious List of our Martyrs.

I will now follow Lord *Bacon* as my Guide, in tracing out such Passions and Affections, as most naturally result from Deformity: for he says, "There certainly is a Consent between the Body and the Mind; and where Nature erreth in the one, she ventureth in the other; and therefore Deformity may be best considered, in this respect, as a Cause which seldom fails of the Effect, and not as a Sign, which is more deceivable; for as there is an Election in Man touching the Frame of his Mind, the Stars of natural Inclination are sometimes eclipsed by the Sun of Discipline and Virtue."[62]

He begins with saying, that "deformed Persons are commonly even with Nature; for as Nature hath done ill by them, so do they by Nature, being for the most part (as the Scripture saith) *void of natural Affection.*" I can neither find out this Passage in Scripture, nor the Reason of it: nor can I give my Assent or Negative to a Proposition, till I am well acquainted with the Terms of it.[63] If by natural Affection is here meant universal Benevolence, and Deformity necessarily implies a want of it, a deformed Person must then be a complete Monster. But however common the Case may be, my own Sensations inform me, that it is not universally true. If by natural Affection is meant a partial Regard for Individuals; I believe the Remark is judicious, and founded in human Nature. Deformed Persons are despised, ridiculed, and ill-treated by others; are seldom Favourites, and commonly most neglected by Parents, Guardians, and Relations: and therefore, as they are not indebted for much Fondness, it is no wonder, if they repay but little. It is the Command of Scripture, *Not to set our Affections on Things below*: it is the Voice of Reason, not to overvalue what we must soon part with: and therefore, to be so fond of others, as not to be able to bear their Absence, or to survive them, is neither a religious or moral Duty; but a childish and womanish Weakness: and I must congratulate deformed Persons, who by Example are early taught another Lesson. And I will now lay open my own Heart to the Reader, that he may judge, if Lord *Bacon*'s Position is verified in me.

I hope it proceeds not from a Malignity of Heart; but I never am much affected with the common Accidents of Life, whether they befall my self or others. I am little moved when I hear of Death, Loss, or Misfortune: I think the Case is common,

(*Tritus, & e medio fortunæ ductus acervo*)[64]

And as it is always likely to happen, I am not surprised when it does. If I see a Person cry or beat his Breast on any such Occasion, I cannot bear him Company, but am not a *Democritus* to laugh at his Folly.[65] I read of Battles and Fields covered with Slain; of cities destroyed by Sword, Famine, Pestilence, and Earthquake; I do not shed a Tear: I suppose it is, because they are the usual Storms, to which the Human Species are exposed, proceeding from the just Judgments of God, or the mistaken and false Principles of Rulers. I read of Persecutions, Tortures, Murders, Massacres; my Compassion for the Sufferers is great, but my Tears are stopped by Resentment and Indignation against the Contrivers and Perpetrators of such horrid Actions. But there are many Things, that bring Tears into my Eyes, whether I will or no: and when I reflect, I am often at a Loss in searching out the secret Source from whence they flow. What makes me weep? (for weep I do) when I read of Virtue or Innocence in Distress; of a good Man, helpless and forsaken, unmoved by the greatest Insults and Cruelties; or courageously supporting himself against Oppression in the Article of Death. I suppose it is, to see Vice triumphant, and Virtue so ill rewarded in this Life. May I judge by my self, I should imagine, that few sincere Christians could read the Sufferings of their Saviour, or *Englishmen* those of *Cranmer, Ridley*, or *Latimer*, without Tears; the first dying to establish his Religion, the last to rescue it from Corruption.[66] When I read of *Regulus*[67] returning to Torment, and *John of France*[68] to Imprisonment, against the Persuasion of Friends, to keep Faith with their Enemies; I weep to think, there is scarce another Instance of such exalted Virtue. Those, who often hear me read, know, that my Voice changes, and my Eyes are full, when I meet with a generous and heroic Saying, Action, or Character, especially of Persons, whose Example or Command may influence Mankind. I weep when I hear a *Titus* say, That he had lost the Day in which he did no Good.[69] When *Adrian*[70] tells his Enemy, That he had escaped by his being Emperor; or *Lewis* XII.[71] That he is not to revenge the Affronts of the Duke of *Orleans*. These are the first Instances that happen to occur to me: I might collect many, too many to insert in this Essay: yet all are but few, compared to Instances of Cruelty and Revenge: perhaps I am concerned, that they are so rare: perhaps too I inwardly grieve, that I am not in a Situation to do the like. I am entertained, but not moved, when I read *Voltaire*'s History of *Charles* XII. but I melt into tears on reading *Hanway*'s Character of his Antagonist *Peter* the Great.[72] The first is the Story of a Madman; the other of a Father, Friend, and Benefactor of his People; whose Character (as the Author observes in the Conclusion of it) will command the Admiration of all succeeding Generations: and I suppose I lament, that God is pleased to advance to Royalty so few such Instruments of Good to Mankind. *Harry* IV. Of *France*[73] had every Quality to make a Prince amiable: Courage, Humanity, Clemency, Generosity,

Affability, Politeness: his Behaviour on every Occasion is charming: and I cannot read the Account of him, given us by his Prime Minister (*Sully*) without Emotion.[74] I do not wonder, if what is reported is true; that at least fifty Persons have written his History; and that he has been celebrated in Poems, and Panegyricks, by above five hundred: there are few such Subjects to be met with; and few Princes, who have so justly deserved the Title of Great.[75] His Grandson had the same Title bestowed on him: but how little did he deserve it![76] He has been celebrated by as many Historiographers and Poets; but they are mostly such as he hired for that Purpose: and none of them, even *Voltaire* himself, will be able to pass him for a great Man on unprejudiced Posterity. Compare him with his Grandfather, you will find him the reverse. *Henry* was bred to Toil and Hardships; *Lewis* in Luxury and Effeminacy. *Henry* pleasant, easy, and affable; *Lewis* formal, haughty, and reserved. *Henry* brave, and exposing himself to all Dangers; *Lewis* cautious, and always in a secure Post. The one gaining Victories by himself, and his own personal Valour; the other by his Generals, and Superiority of Numbers. The one pleased with performing great Actions; the other with being flattered for those which he never performed. The first ambitious of true; and the last of false Glory. *Henry* stabbed by Jesuits; *Lewis* governed by them. The one forgiving Rebels and Assassins; the other encouraging both. *Henry* persecuted; *Lewis* a Persecutor. The first granting Liberty of Conscience; the last taking it away. *Henry* promoting the Silk Manufacture in *France; Lewis* in *England*.[77] One treating his Subjects as his Children; the other as his Slaves. *Henry* bravely asserting his own Rights; *Lewis* basely encroaching on those of his Neighbours. *Henry* extricating his Country from Misery, and laying the Foundation of her Grandeur; *Lewis* squandering her Blood and Treasure, and reducing her from Grandeur to the Brink of Destruction. *Henry* forming Schemes for the perpetual Peace of *Europe; Lewis* perpetually to disturb it. How little is *Lewis* compared to *Henry* the Great!

But to return to my Subject. — I am uneasy, when I see a Dog, a Horse, or any other Animal ill treated; for I consider them as endued with quick Sense, and no contemptible Share of Reason; and that God gave Man Dominion over them, not to play the Tyrant, but to be a good Prince and promote the Happiness of his Subjects. But I am much more uneasy at any Cruelty to my own Species; and heartily with *Procrustis* disciplined in his own Bed, and *Phalaris* in his Bull.[78] A Man bruised all over in a Boxing Match, or cut to Pieces in fighting a Prize, is a shocking Spectacle; and I think I could with less Horror see a thousand fall in Battle, than Human Nature thus depreciated and disgraced. Violence, when exerted in Wantonness or Passion, is Brutality: and can be termed Bravery, only when it is sanctified by Justice and Necessity. A mangled Carcass is not a pleasing Sight. Why therefore do Men pay for it? and the Great Vulgar encourage these Disorders among the Small? It is not Choice, but Affection. As many, who neither love nor understand Musick, go to an Opera to gain the Reputation of Connoiseurs; many go to *Broughton*'s Theater, to avoid the Imputation of being Cowards: but when they are at so much Pains to avoid the Imputation, it raises a Suspicion that they are so.[79]

I have been in a Situation to see not a little of the Pomp and Vanity, as well as of the Necessity and Misery of Mankind: but the last only affect me: and if, as a Magistrate, I am ever guilty of Partiality, it is in favour of the Poor. When I am at Church among my poor, but honest, Neighbours in the Country; and see them serious in performing the Ceremonies prescribed; Tears sometimes steal down my Cheek, on reflecting, that they are doing and hearing many Things they do not understand; while those, who understand them better, neglect them: that they, who labour and live hard, are more thankful to Heaven, than those, who fare luxuriously on the Fruits of their Labour: and are keeping and repeating the fourth Commandment, at the very Instant the others are breaking it.

These are some of the Sensations I feel; which I have freely and fairly disclosed; that the Reader may judge, how far I am an Instance of a deformed Person wanting natural Affection. And I am a good Subject of Speculation; for all in me is Nature: for to own the Truth, I have taken but little Pains (tho' much I ought to have taken) to correct my natural Defects.

Lord *Bacon*'s next Position is, "That deformed Persons are extremely bold. First in their own Defence, as being exposed to Scorn; but in process of Time by a general Habit."—This probably is so among the inferior Sort, who are in the Way of continual Insults: for a Return of Abuse is a natural Weapon of Self-defence; and in some measure justified by the Law of Retaliation: to upbraid a Man with a personal Defect, which he cannot help, is also an immoral Act; and he who does it, has reason to expect no better Quarter, than to hear of Faults, which it was in his own Power not to commit. But I find this Observation far from being verified in my self: an unbecoming Bashfulness has been the Consequence of my ill Figure, and of the worse Management of me in my Childhood. I am always uneasy, when any one looks stedfastly on so bad a Picture: and cannot look with a proper Confidence in the Face of another. I have ever reproached myself with this Weakness, but am not able to correct it.

And it may be a Disadvantage to a Man in the Opinion of those he converses with; for though true Modesty is amiable, the false is liable to Misconstruction; and when a Man is out of Countenance for no Reason, it may be imagined, that he has some bad Reason for being so. In point of Assurance, I am indeed a perfect Riddle to my self: for I, who feel a Reluctance in crossing a Drawing-room, or in opening my Mouth in private Company before Persons with whom I am not well acquainted, find little in delivering my Sentiments in Publick, and exposing my Discourse, often as trifling as my Person, to the Ears of a Thousand. From what Cause this proceeds I know not: it may be, partly from Hopes of wiping off any ill Impressions from my Person by my Discourse; partly from a Sense of doing my Duty; and partly from a Security in publick Assemblies[80] from any gross personal Reflections.

Lord *Bacon* compares the Case of deformed Persons to that of Eunuchs; "in Whom Kings were wont to put great Trust as good Spials and Whisperers; for they that are envious towards all, are more obnoxious and officious towards one."[81] — But with Submission to so good a Judge of Human Nature, I own, I can discover no uncommon Qualifications in them for Spies; and very few Motives to Envy peculiar to themselves. Spies submit to that base and ungenerous Office, either for the Sake of Interest or Power: if for Interest, it is to gratify their Covetousness; if for Power, their Ambition or Revenge: which Passions are not confined to the Eunuch or Deformed; but indiscriminately seize all Classes of Men. Envy too may prompt a Man to mean Actions, in order to bring down the Person envied to his own Level; but if it is on account of Superiority of Fortune, it will operate alike on Men of all Shapes. Eunuchs have but one peculiar Motive to Envy: but that (as Lord *Bacon* expresses it) makes them envious towards all; because it is for a Pleasure, which all but themselves may enjoy. Deformed Persons are deprived only of Beauty and Strength, and therefore those alone are to be deemed the extraordinary Motives to their Envy; for they can no more be beautiful or strong, than Eunuchs be successful Lovers. As to my self; whatever Sparks of Envy might be in my Constitution, they are now entirely extinguished: for by frequent and serious Reflection I have long been convinced of the small Value of most Things which Men value the most.

There is another Passion to which deformed Persons seem to be more exposed, than to Envy: which is Jealousy: for being conscious, that they are less amiable than others, they may naturally suspect, that they are less beloved. I have the Happiness to speak this from Conjecture, and not from Experience: for it was my Lot many Years ago to marry a young Lady, very piously educated, and of a very distinguished Family, and whose Virtues are an Honour to her Family, and her Sex: so that I had never any Trial of my Temper; and can only guess at it by Emotions I have felt in my younger Days; when Ladies have been more liberal of their Smiles to those, whom I thought in every respect, but Person, my Inferiors.

The most useful Inference from all this to a deformed Person, is to be upon his Guard against those Frailties, to which he is more particularly exposed, and to be careful, that the outward Frame do not distort the Soul. *Orandum est,* let us pray, says *Juvenal, ut sit mens sana in corpore sano,* for a sound Mind in a healthy Body;[82] and every deformed Person Should add this Petition, *ut sit mens recta in corpore curvo,* for an upright Mind in a crooked one. And let him frequently apply to himself, this Article of self-examination, *Lenior & melior fis accedente senectâ?*[83] As Age approaches, do your Temper and Morals improve? It is a Duty peculiarly incumbent: for if Beauty adds Grace to Virtue it self, Vice must be doubly hideous in Deformity.

Ridicule and Contempt are a certain Consequence of Deformity: and therefore what a Person cannot avoid, he should learn not to regard. He should bear it like a Man; forgive it as a Christian; and consider it as a Philosopher. And his Triumph will be complete, if he can exceed others in Pleasantry on himself.[84] Wit will give over, when it sees it self out-done: and so will Malice, when it finds it has no Effect: and if a Man's Behaviour afford no Cause of Contempt, it will fall upon those, who condemn him without Cause. It sometimes happens that Persons, with whom I have a slight Acquaintance, will take notice of me on some Days, and overlook me on others: well knowing that they ought to treat one of my Shape, with the precise degree of Ceremony, which suits their present Humour. I will not say, this is a Pleasure; but I can truly say, it is no Mortification. It excites in me no Resentment, but only Speculation. And not able to find out a very good Reason for their Behaviour, I endeavour to find as good a one as I can. I consider with my self, what it is, which makes them at that Juncture of such particular Importance to themselves: and ask my self many Questions of this Sort. Is his Father dead? Has he writ a Play? Has he dined with my Lord Mayor? Has he made a Speech? Has he been presented at Court? Has he been spoke to at a Levee? Has he a new Equipage, or Title? Has he had a good Run? Has he got a Place? Is he going to marry a Fortune? Has he been congratulated on the Performance of his *French* Cook, or his *French* Taylor? Is he admitted of *White's,* or of the Royal Society?[85]—Such are the Topicks of my Speculations; and though I am a Person of no great Penetration, I sometimes hit on the right Cause.

Fine Cloaths attract the Eyes of the Vulgar: and therefore a deformed Person should not assume those borrowed Feathers, which will render him doubly ridiculous. He could scarce expose himself more by dancing at Court; than by appearing the finest there on a Birth-day.[86] Ever since I have arrived at Years of Discretion, I have worn a plain Dress; which, for near thirty years, has been of the same grave Colour; and which I find not the least Inclination to alter. It would be monstrous in me to bestow any Ornament on a Person, which is incapable of it: and should I appear in Lace or Embroidery, my Friends might assign it as no unreasonable Pretence for a Commission of Lunacy against me. — I can scarce forbear digressing on this Subject, when I reflect, what Numbers, who should know better, set a Value upon these Trifles; which are fit Amusements only for Children. If they are pleased with the Finery only; they are no better than Children. If it is to gain Respect: such Respect must come from the Vulgar, and not from Men of Sense. Is it to shew their Quality? it does not, for even Apprentices are fine. Is it to be an Evidence of their Riches? it is not; for the most necessitous are finest, as Taylors know to their Cost. Do their Figure or Reputation depend on their Dress? then they are entirely in the hand of the Taylor: he is the Engineer to guard and defend them; the God to save or destroy: Do they dress to please the Ladies? that is the most reasonable End: yet very few of them but are wiser than to be taken with the Coat instead of the Man: — and what can be taking in a Man, who invades[87] their Province, and appears by his Actions to be one of them? — If it is a Lady that is fond of Finery; I ask her why? If she is a Beauty, she wants no Ornament: if plain, she cannot be transformed. Her Dress indeed may enliven her Poet's Fancy, and save him a Journey to the Sun and Stars for his Similies and Allusions. If the Lady had not put on her Finery; we might have lost this polite and ingenious Stanza.

The adorning thee with so much Art
Is but a barbarous Skill:
'Tis like the poisoning of a Dart,
Too apt before to kill.[88]

Every Mother (like her in *Juvenal*[89]) hath prayed in the Temple of *Venus,* for the most exquisite Beauty in her children. But since the Goddess hath been thus deaf and unkind; I cannot advise any one of my Sect to be her professed Votary: for she will be as little propitious to his Wishes, as she was to his Mother's Prayer. A *Helen* will run away with a *Paris*: but where is the Nymph, that will listen to such a *Corydon?* In vain will he summon the Muses to his Aid, unassisted as he is by the Graces.

His *Sacharissa, Myra, Cloe,* or *Belinda,*[90] may perhaps tickle her Ear, but will never touch her heart:

Not Words alone please her.[91]

Or if (as Waller[92] expresses it) her high Pride should descend to mark his Follies, it is the greatest Honour he can expect: unless in a merry Mood she should take it into her Head to treat him like *Falstaff* or Squire *Slender.*[93] He will be the choicest of *Cupid*'s *April* Fools; and I will not say an egregious Ass, but Camel, to bear his Burthens. But let this be some Consolation to him, that, while he is not suffered to regale on the Sweets of the Hive, he is secured from its Sting.

But, not to make ugly persons out of Love with themselves, I will now exhibit some Advantages arising from Deformity.

Instead of repining, a deformed Person ought to be thankful to Providence for giving him such a Guard to his Virtue and Repose. Thousands are daily ruined by a handsome Person: for Beauty is a Flower, that every one wants to gather in its Bloom, and spare no Pains or Stratagem to reach it. All the Poetical Stories concerning it have their Moral. A *Helen* occasions War and Confusion. The *Hyacinths* and *Ganimedes* are seized on for *Catamites*: the *Endymions* and *Adonis* for Gallants. *Narcissus* can admire no body but himself; and grows old, before he is cured of that Passion. Who is a Stranger to the Story of *Lucretia,* killing herself for her violated Chastitiy? or of *Virginia,* killed by her Father to preserve it? In those Circumstances, says *Juvenal,* she might wish to change Persons with *Rutila,* the only Lady I know among the Ancients celebrated for a Hump-Back.[97] The handsomest Men[95] are chosen for Eunuchs and Gallants: and when they are catched in exercising the last Function, both *Horace* and *Juvenal* inform you of the Penalties and Indignities they undergo.[96] *Silius* was converted by the insatiable Messalina into a Husband:[97] and *Sporus* by the Monster *Nero* into a Wife.[98] The last mentioned Poet shews, that praying for Beauty is praying for a Curse: and *Persius* refuses to join in such a Prayer:[99] and have not I reason to thank my Stars, that have placed me more out of Danger, than even Virtue could; for that could not guard a *Joseph,*[100] an *Hippolytus,*[101] a *Bellerophon,* and others, against the Revenge of slighted Love.

Another great Advantage of Deformity is, that it tends to the Improvement of the Mind. A Man, that cannot shine in his Person, will have recourse to his Understanding: and attempt to adorn that Part of him, which alone is capable of Ornament: when his Ambition prompts him to begin, with *Cowley,* to ask himself this Question,

What shall I do to be for ever known,
And make the Age to come my own?[102]

On looking about him, he will find many Avenues to the Temple of Fame barred against him: but some are still open through that of Virtue: and those, if he has a right Ambition, he will most probably attempt to pass. The more a Man is unactive in his Person, the more his Mind will be at work: and the time which others spend in Action, he will pass in Study and Contemplation: by these he may acquire Wisdom, and by Wisdom Fame. The Name of *Socrates* is as much sounded, as those of *Alexander* and *Caesar*, and is recorded in much fairer Characters. He gained Renown by Wisdom and Goodness; they by Tyranny and Oppression: he by instructing; they by destroying Mankind: and happy it is, that their evil Deeds were confined to their Lives; while he continues to instruct us to this Day. A deformed Person will naturally consider, where his Strength and his Foible lie; and as he is well acquainted with the last, he will easily find out the first; and must know, that (if it is any where) it is not, like *Sampson*'s, in the Hair; but must be in the Lining of the Head. He will say to himself, I am weak in Person: unable to serve my Country in the Field; I can acquire no military Glory: but I may, like *Socrates*, acquire Reputation by Wisdom and Probity: let me therefore be wise and honest. My Figure is very bad: and I should appear but ill as an Orator, either in the Pulpit or at the Bar: let me therefore pass my Time in my Study, either in reading what may improve myself, or in writing what may entertain or instruct others. I have not the Strength of *Hercules*; nor can I rid the World of so many Monsters: but perhaps I may get rid of some my self. If I cannot draw out *Cacus* from his Den; I may pluck the Villain from my own Breast. I cannot cleanse the Stables of *Augeas*; but I may cleanse my own Heart from Filth and Impurity: I may demolish the *Hydra* of Vices within me; and should be careful too, that while I lop off one, I do not suffer more to grow up in its stead.[103] Let me be serviceable in any way that I can: and if I am so, it may in some measure be owing to my Deformity. Which at least should be a Restraint on my Conduct, lest my Conduct make me more deformed.

Few Persons have a House entirely to their Mind; or the Apartment in it disposed as they could wish. And there is no deformed Person, who does not wish, that his Soul had a better Habitation: which is sometimes not lodged according to its Quality. Lord *Clarendon* says of Sir *Charles Cavendish* (Brother to the Marquis of *Newcastle*) that he was a Man of the noblest and largest Mind, though of the least and most inconvenient Body, that lived.[104] And every body knows, that the late Prince of

Orange had many amiable Qualities. Therefore in Justice to such Persons I must suppose, that they did not repine, that their Tenements were not in a more regular Style of Architecture. And let every deformed Person comfort himself with reflecting; that tho' his Soul hath not the most convenient and beautiful Apartment, yet that it is habitable: that the Accommodation will serve in an Inn upon the Road: that he is but Tenant for Life, or (more properly) at Will: and that, while he remains in it, he is in a State to be envied by the Deaf, the Dumb, the Lame, and the Blind.

When I die, I care not what becomes of the contemptible Carcass, which is the Subject of this Essay. I wonder at the Weakness of some of the old Patriarchs, that provided burying Places, that their Bones might be gathered to their Fathers. Doth one Clod of Earth delight in the Neighbourhood of another? or is there any Conversation in the Grave? It must have been a Joke in Sir *Samuel Garth*, when he ordered himself and Lady to be buried at *Harrow on the Hill*: one of his Strength of Mind could have no Superstition of that Sort.[105] It is of no Consequence where the Body rots: whether it rots immediately, or be preserved a few Years: or whether it be devoured by Birds or Beasts, or placed in a sumptuous Tomb. If a Man doth not provide himself a Monument by his Actions, and embalm his Memory in Virtue; the lying Marble will decay; and then his Memorial (even in that little Corner) will perish;

Quandoquidem data sunt ipsis quoque fata sepulchris.[106]

The *Pharoahs* are stolen from their Pyramids; and their Mummies dispersed thro' the World, only as idle Curiosities. And tho' the Pyramids are more durable than common Sepulchers; yet their History is already unknown, and they must in the End undergo the same Fate. *Mr. Addison*[107] admires the Humanity of *Cyrus* (or rather of *Xenophon*) in ordering his Body to be buried in the Earth, that it might be useful in manuring it. My Flesh will afford but little Manure: but in another Respect my Carcass may be of eminent Service to Mankind: and therefore if I should die intestate, or not mention it in my Will; let the World take this as my dying Request. As I have for some Years been afflicted with the Stone,[108] and owe the Preservation and Ease of Life since to the continued taking of great Quantities of Soap, I desire my Body may be opened and examined by eminent Surgeons; that Mankind may be informed of its Effect. And if a Stone should be found in my Bladder (as I imagine there will) I desire it may be preserved among Sir *Hans Sloane*'s Collection.[109] — Until that Time comes, I hope to employ the little Remainder of Life in Pursuits not unbecoming a rational Creature.

My C A S E.

For many Years red Sand constantly came from me without Pain or Inconvenience. About nine Years ago I began to be uneasy: and before twelve Months had passed, was so much out of Order, that I could no longer ride; the Motion of a Coach grew insupportable; and that of a Chair, or Walking, was generally attended with bloody Water.

The Regimen.

I took Mrs. *Stephens*'s Medicine in the solid Form, three Ounces a Day, for about five Years; when I changed it for the same Quantity of Castile Soap; which about a Year since I reduced to two Ounces; and lately to one Ounce, with about a Pint of Lime-Water mixt with Milk; being willing to regain my Liberty, as far as is consistent with Ease and Safety.[110] This Regimen I have incessantly pursued; except some few Days that I have purposely omitted it, to observe the Consequences of such Omission;

The Effects

Whilst I pursue this Regimen, I never discharge red Sand; whenever I omit it for a few days, I constantly do. By a steady Perseverance in it, my particular Complaint has been gradually diminished; and my Health in general improved. I believe I could now ride, tho' I have not tried. I seldom feel any Uneasiness in a Coach; and when I do, it is inconsiderable; tho' sometimes (but very rarely) it is attended with bloody Water. And the Motion of a Chair or Walking do not affect me. In short, I have exchanged Pain for Ease, and Misery for Comfort: and had it not been for this Medicine, I should not have been now alive to have told my Story.

My Conclusions are these.

1. Mrs. *Stephens*'s Medicine or Castile Soap are safe Remedies: and three Ounces may be taken every Day for Years together (and probably during Life) without any ill Consequence.

2. That Health in general will improve by their Use: for by their cleansing Quality, I imagine, they better prepare the Stomach for Digestion, and the Intestines for Chylification.

3. They are Preventives of the Stone; either by hindering the Generation or Formation of those Particles of which it is composed, or by facilitating the discharge of them before Concretion. And I am persuaded, that by taking them, Persons, who have not that Distemper, will be secured from it; and those, who have it, from growing worse. And if

45

on lessening my Quantity I again find the Appearance of red Sand, I will increase it again to a Quantity sufficient to prevent it.

4. They are Lithontriptics. Of this I have often had ocular Proof: and the discharged Fragments are softened; and their Parts more easily separated.

5. They are Lenitives: where the Stone is not entirely discharged: so that when a compleat Cure is not obtained, Ease may; as I have happily experienced. But from what Cause this proceeds, let Physicians enquire and determine.

I believe, Men scarce differ so much in the Temper of their Bodies, as of their Minds: and tho' many Cases may be very unlike my own, I am persuaded, that a regular Use of this Medicine would for the most part be as beneficial to others as to my self. Persons, with whom it disagrees, in other respects, are excluded from this Benefit: as the Intemperate are from the Benefit of this or any other Medicine.

I have for a long Course of Years abstained from all strong Liquors; but drink every thing that is small. I can eat any thing, but not much; and like the most common Diet best. I prefer most things to Flesh; and of Flesh the whitest. I never altered my common Diet on Account of this Medicine; or the times of my Meals, which have ever been very irregular. I have always taken an Ounce at a time; sometimes before, sometimes at, and sometimes after Meals: and I have often made a Meal of the Medicine itself, only with a Glass of small Liquor (of any sort) and a little Bread, which I have always taken with it. I generally took the three Ounces at proper Intervals; and sometimes at very short ones. This Medicine has always agreed with me; and I never once felt it on my Stomach, or any other Inconvenience from it. And I think it my Duty to omit no Opportunity of publishing its Virtues to the World.

POSTSCRIPT.

Since I finished this Essay, I am in Doubt whether I ought not to change the Title. For I have heard of a very ingenious Performance, called *The Analysis of Beauty*, which proves incontestably, that it consists in Curve Lines; I congratulate my Fraternity; and hope for the future the Ladies will esteem them *Des Beaux Garçons*.[111]

POST–POSTSCRIPT

I Wonder, that in the first Edition of this Essay, I forgot to mention some Inconveniences I suffer of a very grievous Nature; and which have a Right to a Place in Pages 18 and 19.[112]

When I am in a Coach with a Fair Lady, I am hid by Silk and Whalebone. When I sit next her at Table, my Arm is so pinioned, I can neither help her nor myself. We are deprived of the Pleasure of seeing each other: and she would scarce know I was there, if she did not sometimes hear me under her Wing. I am in Purgatory on the Confines of Paradise. I therefore beg one Favour, and which she may grant with Honour; that (since I despair of supplanting her Lap-dog[*]) she will allow me a Cushion to raise me above such Misfortunes.

FINIS

NOTES

INTRODUCTION

1. Francis Tutté, "Preface" in *The Works of William Hay, Esq.*, (London: J. Nichols, 1794), iii-iv.

2. Tutté, iii.

3. Tutté, iv-v.

4. Stephen Taylor and Clyve Jones, *Tory and Whig: The Parliamentary Papers of Edward Harley, 3rd Earl of Oxford, and William Hay, M.P. for Seaford 1716-1753* (Woodbridge, Suffolk: Boydell Press, 1998), lxii.

5. Taylor and Jones, lxiii.

6. Henry, Hay's youngest son, predeceased him in October, 1754. His second son, William, died violently in India in 1763. His eldest son, Thomas, served as M.P. for Lewes, 1768-1780 (Taylor and Jones, lxiii). Hay's nephew and biographer, the Rev. Francis Tutté, inherited Glyndebourne on the death of Frances, William Hay's younger daughter. Hay's daughters bore the expense of the publication of the two volume *Works* in 1794 to which Tutté affixed a biographical preface (*Dictionary of National Biography*, s.v. "Hay, William.").

7. Taylor and Jones, lxiii.

8. *Fugitive Pieces on Various Subjects by Several Authors. In two volumes* (London: R Dodsley, 1761, 1762, 1765, 1771).

9. Tutté, x.

10. Hay, *Works*, 112.

11. Tutté, vi-xi.

12. Some comments in this section of the introduction also appear in *Prose Studies* (2004).

13. Spender, "In the Bodyshop: Human Exhibition in Early Modern England," in *"Defects": Engendering the Modern Body*, ed. Helen Deutsch and Felicity Nussbaum (Ann Arbor: University of Michigan Press, 2000), 115, 116. Davis, "Dr. Johnson, Amelia, and the Discourse of Disability in the Eighteenth Century," in *"Defects*," 60.

14. Abbot Quillet, *Callipaediae* [sic] or *An Art how to have Handsome Children Written in Latin by the Abbot Quillet. To which is Added, Paedotrophiae; Or, the Art of Nursing and Breeding up Children*, trans. John Morphew (London, 1710), 1.

15. Lady Mary Wortley Montagu is typical of Alexander Pope's enemies who mocked his hunchback as the "Emblem of . . . [his] crooked Mind,/Mark'd on. . . [his] Back, like *Cain*, by God's own Hand ("Verses Address'd the IMITATOR of the FIRST SATIRE of the Second Book of Horace" in *Essays and Poems and* Simplicity, *a Comedy*, ed. Robert Halsband and Isobel Grundy [Oxford: Clarendon Press, 1993], lines 110-11).

16. David T. Mitchell and Sharon L. Snyder, *Narrative Prosthesis: Disability and the Dependencies of Discourse* (Ann Arbour: University of Michigan Press, 2000), 48.

[17] See Lennard Davis, "The End of Identity Politics and the Beginning of Dismodernism" in *Bending Over Backwards: Disability, Dismodernism and Other Difficult Positions* (New York: New York University Press, 2002), 9-32.

[18] For a summary of competing accounts, see Henri-Jacques Stiker, *A History of Disability*, trans. William Sayers (Ann Arbor: University of Michigan Press, 1999), 91-119.

[19] Paré, *On Monsters and Marvels*, trans. Janis L. Pallister (Chicago: University of Chicago Press, 1982), 3-4.

[20] Pierre Boiastuau, "Preface" in *Certaine secrete wonders of nature,containing a descriptio[n] of sundry strange things, seming monstrous in our eyes and iudgement, bicause we are not priuie to the reasons of them. Gathered out of diuers learned authors as well Greeke as Latine, sacred as prophane*, trans. Edward Fenton (London, 1569), n.p.

[21] Sir Francis Bacon, *The Essayes or Counsels, Civill and Morall*, ed. Michael Kiernan (Cambridge, MA: Harvard University Press, 1985), 134.

[22] Described by G.J. Barker-Benfield as a "great watchword of the eighteenth century," the improvement of society through the reformation of manners was the central goal of the myriad conduct books published in the period for middle class men and women (*The Culture of Sensibility* [Chicago: University of Chicago Press, 1992], 2).

[23] Review of *Deformity: An Essay*, by William Hay. *The Gentleman's Magazine* (1753), 593. In a letter to John Nichols in 1813 George Hardinge praises Hay's "humour, wit, ingenuity, elegant style, fancy, and good sense" calling his "playful ridicule upon his own deformity" unexampled (*Literary Anecdotes of the Eighteenth Century*, ed. John Nichols, vol. 8 [London, 1814], 520).

[24] *Dictionary of the English Language*, 2 vols. (London: Thomas Tegg, 1831).

[25] Hay, *Deformity*,.

[26] *Dictionary of National Biography*, s.v. "Broughton, John."

[27] David T. Mitchell and Sharon L. Snyder, introduction to *The Body and Physical Difference*, ed. David T. Mitchell and Sharon L. Snyder (Ann Arbor: University of Michigan Press, 1997), 15.

[28] Hay, *Deformity*,.

[29] Bacon, "Of Deformity," 133-134.

[30] For a discussion of the limitations of the autobiographical narrative of disability see Mitchell and Snyder, *Body*, "Introduction," 17 and Lennard J. Davis, *Enforcing Normalcy:Disability, Deafness, and the Body* (London: Verso Press, 1995), 3-4. G. Thomas Couser has written extensively on illness narratives but overlooks Hay's essay as an early example of this mode. See *Recovering Bodies: Illness, Disability, and Life Writing* (Madison, WI: University of Wisconsin Press, 1997).

[31] For a discussion of men's relation to the culture of sensibility see Barker-Benfield, *Culture*, 37-103. See also Anne C. Vila, *Enlightenment and Pathology: Sensibility in the Literature and Medicine of Eighteenth-Century France* (Baltimore: Johns Hopkins University Press, 1998) and Janet Todd, *Sensibility: An Introduction* (London: Methuen, 1986).

[32] Hay, *Deformity*,.

[33] Bacon, "Of Deformity," 134.

[34] Hay, *Deformity*,.

[35] See *Spectator* 17 (*The Spectator*, ed. Donald F. Bond [Oxford: Clarendon Press, 1965]).

[36] Hay, *Deformity*,.

[37] Felicity Nussbaum, "Dumb Virgins, Blind Ladies, and Eunuchs: Fictions of Defect," in *"Defects,"* 50.

[38] Hay, Deformity,.

[39] See, for example, "Epistle 97," *Epistles for the Ladies*, vol. 2 (London, 1750), 103-106. The letter-writer, Mira, urges her correspondent, Fidelia, to avoid the masquerade because it is "not only foolish, but immoral" and affords "a Sanction to all the Indecencies of Speech" (104).

[40] Of the three editions, the second and third include this post-postscript introduced with the statement that the "Inconveniences" described belong on "Pages 18 and 19" (84) but in neither is the material inserted into the body of the text. The "fourth edition" published in Dublin by George Faulkner also in 1754 appears to be a reprint of the first edition as it lacks the post-post script.

[41] I am indebted to Brycchan Carey for his suggestion that Hay refers, here, to Francis Williams (Brycchan Carey, email to C18-L, September 10, 2003). Born in Jamaica of "free black parents about the year 1700," Williams was sent to England under the sponsorship of the Duke of Montagu to receive a gentleman's education at a grammar school and Cambridge University. Montagu wished to prove that Black people had the same capacities to learn as white people. Following his studies, Williams returned to Jamaica where Montagu tried to have him appointed to the governor's council "but the governor, Edward Trelawney, found him unacceptable" (Peter Fryer, *Staying Power: The History of Black People in Britain* [London: Pluto Press, 1984], 421).

[42] Boaistuau records the ancient belief that catching sight of "monstrous creatures" foretold misfortune. His examples are of Hadrian and the "soldiers of Brutus" who believed they would soon die having seen, respectively, "a Moore and an Ethiopian" (*Certaine secrete wonders*, 15r).

[43] Eileen Spring, *Law, Land, and Family: Aristocratic Inheritance in England, 1300 to 1800* (Chapel Hill, NC: University of North Carolina, 1993).

[44] Richard B. Schwartz reports that in 1764 in London 60% of children died before the age of five (*Daily Life in Johnson's London* [Madison, WI: University of Wisconsin Press, 1983], 143). For examples of manuals advising parents how to prevent and correct deformities, see, for example, Quillet, *Callipaediae*. A translation in heroic couplets of the Latin original, *Callipaediae*, in its first book, warns the old, miserly husband that if he marries a young woman she will undoubtedly bear him bastards, for fear of birthing his "deform'd or sickly Child" (23). As a consequence, "Thy Hoards descend to these, and theirs shall be/The Lands, which from thy Fathers fell to Thee/These thy rich Pastures shall enjoy, and these,/A Foreign Race, thy Ancient Seat possess" (24). The causes of children's deformities were more often ascribed to the force of pregnant women's imaginations; see especially Daniel Turner, *De Morbis Cutaneis. A Treatise of Diseases Incident to the Skin. In Two Parts* (London, 1714). The view persisted even into the nineteenth century in spite of James Augustus Blondel's refutation in 1727. For a discussion

of this debate, see Julia Epstein, *Altered Conditions: Disease, Medicine, and Storytelling* (New York: Routledge, 1995), 123-156.

45 Boiastuau, *Certaine secrete wonders*, 12v.

46 Boiastuau, *Certaine secrete wonders*, 69v.

47 Translated into English in 1743 and aimed at parents and caregivers of children, this book was later slightly abridged and republished with a "particular view to the service of the ladies" in 1786 as *Hebe; or, The Art of Preserving Beauty, and Correcting Deformity; Being a Complete Treatise on the Various Defects of the human Body, with the most approved Methods of Prevention and Cure; and the Preservation of Health and Beauty in General* (London: J. Walker, 1786). Nussbaum errs in treating these two as different works ("Dumb Virgins," 34-35).

48 Nicolas de Bois-Regard Andry, *Orthopaedia: Or, the Art of Correcting and Preventing Deformities in Children: By such Means, as may easily be put in Practice by Parents themselves, and all such as are employed in Educating Children. To Which is added, a Defence of the Orthopaeia, by way of Supplement, by the Author*, 2 vols. (London: A. Millar, 1743), 36-37.

49 Andry, *Orthopaedia* ,72.

50 Andry, *Orthopaedia*, 38.

51 Hay, *Deformity*,.

52 Hay slightly misquotes John Dryden's poem "To My Honour'd Kinsman John Driden." An encomium to a cousin who provided financial help to Dryden, the poem advocates avoiding both marriage and physicians. The lines read: "The wise for cure on exercise depend / God never made his work for man to mend" (94-95).

53 Hay probably refers to his parents who died in his infancy; ironically, his youngest son died of a "fatal disorder on his lungs" only months after the essay's publication (Tutté, "Preface," xvi).

54 Bacon, "Of Deformity," 134.

55 Bacon, "Of Deformity," 134.

56 Hay, *Deformity*,.

57 A quality with significant value in the eighteenth century, "wit" included in its many meanings intelligence, learning, and clever use of language.

58 Hay cites the proverb *Incidit in Scyllam cupiens vitare Carybden* (*Deformity*,). (Wishing to avoid Carybdis, he ran upon Scylla.)

59 In March 1740, Parliament paid Joanna Stephens the remarkable sum of £5,000 to publish her remedy, sparking a scientific controversy that continued throughout the eighteenth century. See Arthur J. Viseltear, "Joanna Stephens and the Eighteenth-Century Lithontriptics; A Misplaced Chapter in the History of Therapeutics," *Bulletin of the History of Medicine* 42 (1968): 299-220. Contemporary discussion includes David Hartley, *Ten Cases of Persons who have taken Mrs. Stephens's Medicines for the Stone* (London, 1738); James Kirkpatrick, An Account of the Success of Mrs. Stephens's Medicines for the Stone (Belfast, 1739); Joanna Stephens, *A Most Excellent Cure for the Stone and Gravel* (London, 1740?); Stephen Hales, *An Account of Some Experiments and Observations on Mrs. Stephens's Medicines for Dissolving the Stone* (London, 1740); Richard Gem, *An Account of the Remedy for the Stone,*

Lately Published in England (London, 1741); James Parsons, *A Description of the Human Urinary Bladder, and Parts Belonging to it* (London, 1742); John Rutty, *A Particular Account of Mrs. Stephens's Method of Preparing and Giving the Medicine for the Stone and Gravel* (London, 1750).

ESSAY

[1] The inscription on the golden apple in the Judgement of Paris, the outcome of which was the Trojan War.

[2] Michel Eyquem, seigneur de Montaigne, 1533-92. His *Essais* were published in three volumes and in various states, 1580-95. Hay's personal essay is modeled on the genre developed by Montaigne.

[3] [Hay's note: The Marquis of Halifax in a Letter to Charles Cotton, Esq; who translated *Montaigne's* Essays, says, it is the Book in the World, with which he is best entertained: and that Montaigne did not write for Praise; but to give the World a true Picture of himself and of Mankind.] The letter to which Hay refers appears after the "Advertisement" in the third edition of Cotton's translation (*Essays of Michael Seigneur de Montaigne*, Trans. Charles Cotton [London, 1700] n.p.).

[4] [Hay's note: *Vertu Naïve*, an Expression of *Montaigne*; and which *Fontenelle* puts into his Mouth in his Dialogue with *Socrates*.] The phrase "vertu naïfve" appears in Montaigne's "De la Vanité," volume three of the Essais. In Bernard le Bovier de Fontenelle's *Dialogues des Morts Anciens avec des Modernes* (1683), the character Montaigne tells Socrates he wishes to understand Socrates' unique quality of "vertu naïfve" (*Oeuvres Complètes*, Ed. G.B. Depping. Tome 2. [Genève: Slatkine Reprints, 1968], 189).

[5] Anatomized: opened to detailed analysis in the style of Robert Burton's *The Anatomy of Melancholy* (1651).

[6] This statement of purpose derives from Montaigne's "Au Lecteur" which explains, "[q]ue si j'eusse esté entre ces nations qu'on dict vivre encore sous la douce liberté des premières lois de la nature, je t'asseure que je m'y fusse tres-volontiers peint tout entier, et tout nud. Ainsi, lecteur, je suis moy-mesmes la matiere de mon livre: ce n'est pas raison que tu employes ton loisir en un subject si frivole et si vain" (*Essais*, ed. Albert Thibaudet [Bruges: Librairie Gallimard, 1950], 25). Charles Cotton's translation (1630-1687) follows that by John Florio (1553?-1625) in omitting this prefatory note.

[7] [Hay's note: In the Beginning of his Treatise on the Sublime.] The opening sentences of Longinus's (first century A.D.) treatise on aesthetics, *On the Sublime*, criticize Gaius Plinius Cecilius Secundus (230-168 B.C.) for clumsily listing examples of the sublime without considering the means by which it is produced. See Longinus, *On the Sublime* in *Classical Literary Criticism*, trans. T.S. Dorsch (London: Penguin Books, 1965), 99. Longinus says he aims at surpassing Cecilius by writing well about the sublime, whereas Hay wishes to reverse Cecilius's example by writing beautifully about deformity.

[8] [Hay's note: In his Essay on Criticism.] Alexander Pope praises Longinus as an ardent but just critic "Whose *own Example* strengthens all his Laws,/And *Is himself*

that great *Sublime* he draws" (*Essay on Criticism* in *Pastoral Poetry and An Essay on Criticism*, ed. E. Audra and Aubrey Williams [London: Methuen & Co., 1961], lines 679-80).

9 [Hay's note: It was a disobliging Stroke to a Lady; but it was said of Mademoiselle de Gournai, that to vindicate her Honour from Reflection, she need only prefix her Picture to her book. *General Dictionary, under the Word (Gournai).*] The anecdote appears in Pierre Bayle's *A General Dictionary, Historical and Critical*, 10 vols. (London, 1734-41), 2.585. Marie le Jars de Gournay (1565-1645), writer, editor of Montaigne, and early modern feminist, was a frequent target of jokes perpetrated by her literary enemies in Paris. Throughout the 1630s she appears as a character in satires of the Académie Française.

10 In proposing this origin for his hunchback, Hay follows medical opinion of his time that deformities were primarily caused by the pregnant woman's imagination leaving its impression upon the foetus. See introduction.

11 Esop: Aesop (sixth century BCE), traditionally, composer of Greek fables; Prince of Orange: William III (1650-1702) who ascended the British throne in 1689; Marshal Luxemburg: François Henri De Montmorency-Bouteville, Duke of Luxemburg (1628-1695), marshal of France whose forces met those of William III; Lord Treasurer Salisbury: Robert Cecil, first Earl of Salisbury (1563-1612) and Lord Treasurer to James I; Scarron: Paul Scarron, French poet and dramatist (1610-1660) paralysed after an illness contracted in 1638; Alexander Pope (1688-1744).

12 [Hay's note: *Tam mala Thersiten prohibebat forma latere,/ Quam pulchrâ Nireus conspiciendus erat. Ovid. Epistulae Ex Ponto* 13. L. 4]. Trans: Just as Thersites's ugliness prevented him from hiding his appearance, so Nireus was conspicuous on account of his beauty (4.13.16-17). In this letter pleading for Carus's assistance in securing a change of exile, Ovid praises his friend's style for its dignity equal to its heroic subject, Herakles. He describes his own style as remarkable for its faults and follows with the comparison between Thersites and Nireus (see *Iliad* 2.673-74).

13 [Hay's note: George Buck, Esq; who in his *History of Richard the Third* endeavours to represent him as a Prince of much better Shape (both of Body and Mind) than he had been generally esteemed. And Bishop Nicolson calls Buck a more candid Composer of Annals than Sir Thomas More. See his *Historical Library.*] Hay refers to *The History of the Life and Reigne of Richard the Third* (London: W. Wilson, 1647) originally written by Sir George Buck (d. 1623) but edited and published by his great-nephew, George Buck, esq. Buck asserts of Richard, "[h]e was of a mean or lowe compact, but without disproportion & unevenness either in lineaments or parts (as his serverall Pictures present him.) His aspect had most of the Souldier in it; so his natural inclination" (p. 148). The assessment of Buck's account by William Nicolson, Bishop of Carlisle (1655-1727) continues "[v]arious are the Censures which have pass'd upon this Work" (*The English, Scotch and Irish Historical Libraries* [London: G. Strahan, 1736], 84).

14 [Hay's note: See *Plutarch* in the Life of *Lycurgus.*] According to Lycurgus's reforms, deformed children were buried in a cave near Mount Taygetus for the child's and the public's good "since Nature had denied it the means of happiness in its own particular, by not giving it health nor strength sufficient to make it ser-

viceable to the publick" (Plutarch, "The Life of Lycurgus," *Lives*, trans. Chetwood [London: Jacob Tonson, 1700], 167).

15 Agesilaus, a popular Spartan king, had one leg shorter than the other.

16 The quotation is slightly altered from John Dryden's "To My Honour'd Kinsman, John Driden": "God never made his Work, for Man to mend" (95). (John Dryden, *Works*, ed. Vinton A. Dearing, Vol. 7 [Berkeley: University of California Press, 2000],199).

17 [Hay's note: In his Epistle to Dr. *Arbuthnot* are these Lines.
"The Morals blacken'd, when the Writings 'scape,
The libell'd Person, and the pictur'd Shape, &c.".] Lines 352-53.

18 *Chair*: in this context, an enclosed chair or covered vehicle for one person, carried on two poles by two men. (OED).

19 [Hay's note: Odi profanum vulgus, & arceo. Ode I.L.3] Trans: "I hate the uninitiate crowd and keep them far away" (1-2). (Horace, *The Odes and Epodes*, Trans. C. E. Bennet [Cambrdige, MA: Harvard University Press, 1968],169).

20 Hay slightly misquotes the passage: "There is no terror, Cassius, in your threats;/ For I am arm'd so strong in honesty/That they pass by me as the idle wind/Which I respect not" (*Julius Caesar* 4.3.66-69).

21 [Hay's note: I might add another Bon Mont [sic] of *Socrates*; when asked, how he could bear the Noses [sic] and Ill-manners of *Xantippe*, he replied, They that live in a trading Street are not disturbed at the Passage of Carts. See the Spectator, No. 479.] Hay remembers a passage in Diogenes Laertius' *Life of Socrates* in which Socrates asks, "Should I have taken the law of a donkey, supposing that he had kicked me?" (Vol. 1, trans. R.D. Hicks [Cambridge, MA: Harvard University Press, 1972], 153).

22 William III.

23 I am indebted to Brycchan Carey for his suggestion that Hay may refer to Francis Williams ("Re: Query about African presence in Britain ca. 1700-1750." Online posting. 10 Sept. 2003 Eighteenth Century Interdisciplinary Discussion <http:// lists.psu.edu/cgi-bin/wa?A2=ind0309&L=c18-L&P=R6134&I=-3>). Born in Jamaica of "free black parents about the year 1700," Williams was sent to England under the sponsorship of the Duke of Montagu to receive a gentleman's education at a grammar school and Cambridge University. Montagu wished to prove that black people had the same ability to learn as white people. Following his studies, Williams returned to Jamaica where Montagu tried to have him appointed to the governor's council "but the governor, Edward Trelawney, found him unacceptable" (Peter Fryer, *Staying Power: The History of Black People in Britain* [London: Pluto Press, 1984], 421).

24 [Hay's note: Spectator, No. 17.] Steele's essay, published March 20, 1711, recounts the formation in Oxford of the "Ugly Club," an "ill-favoured Fraternity" of twelve fellows elected for their compliance with the group's "Act of Deformity."

25 emended from "stride" in the second edition.

26 Richard Onslow (1697-1760), MP for Guildford 1727-60 and brigadier-general, 1742-60. His brother was Arthur Onslow (1691-1768), M.P. for Surrey, 1727-61 and Speaker of the House of Commons, 1728-61.

27 Named for the village in southwest Germany where it took place, the battle of Dettingen occurred on June 27, 1743 during the War of the Austrian Succession.

George II was present at the combat along with his second son, William Augustus, Duke of Cumberland.

28 In the battle of Fontenoy on May 11, 1745 the French were the victors. His Royal Highness is William Augustus, Duke of Cumberland.

29 i.e. Whig.

30 John West, Lord Delawar, 7th baron (1693-1766; succ. 1723).

31 Abolished in England in 1972, quarter sessions is a court of limited criminal and civil jurisdiction, and of appeal, held quarterly by the justices of peace in the counties in England and Ireland (OED). Hay became a justice of the peace in the eastern division of Sussex in 1727.

32 This story appears in *Spectator* 17, "The Ugly Club."

33 According to the "Life of Æsop" that prefaces Samuel Richardson's 1740 edition of the *Fables*, Æsop was convicted in Delphos on a trumped up charge of theft and executed by being pushed off a rock where "he was dashed to pieces with the fall" (Samuel Richardson, "The Life of Æsop" *Fables*. [London, 1740] xxxii.)

34 William III died of fever, March 8, 1702, having been thrown by his horse two weeks before.

35 [Hay's note: See Historical Memoirs of Queen *Elizabeth*, by *Francis Osborn*, Esq;] William Cecil, 1st Baron Burghley (or Burleigh) (1520-1598) and Robert Cecil, 1st Earl of Salisbury (1653-1612).

36 Alexander Pope, the father of the poet, died in 1717 at age 71 but was not deformed.

37 Hay was orphaned at age five, his father dying in 1697 and his mother, 1700.

38 Proverbial: Wishing to avoid Carybdis, he runs upon Scylla.

39 [Hay's note: *Non est vivere, sed valere, vita.* — Mart. L. 6 Ep. 70] Translated by Hay as "[L]ife is only life, when we are well" (*Select Epigrams of Martial* [London, 1755], 39).

40 Luigi Cornaro (1475-1566) was the author of *The Sure and Certain Method of Attaining a Long and Healthful Life*, a popular treatise on temperance mentioned by Addison in Spectator 195. Having been made ill by dissipated living until the age of 40, Cornaro restricted his caloric intake and lived another 51 years.

41 Small beer had low alcohol content, being fermented from weaker wort than strong beer.

42 A famous athlete of the later sixth century B.C., Milo of Croton in southern Italy was six times victorious in wrestling in both the Olympian and Pythian games. "He is said to have carried a heifer down the course, killed it with one blow, and eaten it all in one day. Trying to rend a tree asunder he was caught in the cleft and eaten alive by wolves" (Simon Hornblower and Antony Spawforth, *The Oxford Classical Dictionary*, 3rd ed. [Oxford: Oxford University Press, 1996]).

43 Slack and Broughton: John Broughton (1705-1789), a London pugilist patronised by the elite including the Duke of Cumberland, was blinded by Slack in the fight that ended his career on April 11, 1750. (DNB).

44 *Field of false Honour*: the duel. See Steele's papers on duelling in *The Tatler*, numbers 25, 26, 28, 29, 31, 38 and 39.

[45] Hay suggests that a person of very short stature could not be seen by bystanders positioned behind the bar separating them from the courtroom.

[46] A mountain in central Greece, Parnassus is associated with the worship of Apollo and the Muses. Elis, a Greek state in northwest Peloponnesus, comprises a plain in which the Olympian games were held. Pindar (518-after 446 B.C.), a Greek lyric poet, was famous for his Epinician Odes written to honour the victors in the four great Pan-Hellenic games, Olympian, Pythian, Nemean, and Isthmian. (*The Oxford Companion to Classical Literature*, ed. M.C. Howatson [Oxford: Oxford University Press, 1989]).

[47] In his essay "Of Ceremonies and Respects," Bacon writes "it doth much adde, to a Mans Reputation, and is, (as Queene Isabella said) Like perpetuall Letters Commendatory, to have good Formes" (*The Essayes or Counsels, Civill and Morall*, ed. Michael Kiernan [Cambridge, MA: Harvard Univeristy Press, 1985], 157).

[48] [Hay's note: His Essay on Beauty]

[49] Pedro de la Gasca (1485-1567 ?) priest and colonial administrator of Peru, 1547-1550.

[50] [Hay's note: His Essay on Deformity]

[51] [Hay's note: *De Augmentis Scientiarum*, L. 8 c. 2.] This passage appears in Gilbert Watts's 1640 translation : "Which kinde of fortified carriage together with a prompt and prepared resolution to vindicate a mans selfe from scorne, is imposed upon some by accident and a kinde of an inevitable necessity, for somewhat inherent in their person or fortune, as we see it in Deformed Persons and Bastards, and in Persons any way disgrac'd , so that such natures, if they have any good parts commonly they succeed with good felicity" (Francis Bacon, *Of the Advancement and Proficience of Learning; or, The Partitions of Sciences*, trans. Gilbert Watts [Oxford: Leon Lichfield, 1640], 413).

[52] [Hay's note: I suppose what *Cambden* says of Lord *Burleigh*'s comely and pleasing Aspect, relates to his Countenance only.] Osborn reports that Elizabeth I, choosing counselors solely for their wisdom, overlooked "a mean Birth, and Crooked Person, as it chanced in a Father and Son of the *Cecils*, both incomparable for Prudence." An earlier passage ascribes to Elizabeth's reputed practice of hiring only "persons of stature, strength and birth" for her household servants the motivation of displaying for foreign visitors the strength and virility of England. (*Memoirs on Queen Elizabeth. The Works of Francis Osborn Esq.* [London, 1701], 333). In Robert Norton's translation of Camden's history of Elizabeth I, Burleigh's countenance is described as "undistempered" (William Camden, *Annales; or, The History of the Most Renowned and Victorious Princesse Elizabeth, late Queen of England*, trans. Robert Norton, 3rd ed., [London, 1635], 494).

[53] [Hay's note: Historical Memoirs of K. *James.*] *Memoirs on King James. The Works of Francis Osborn Esq.* (London, 1701), 412.

[54] The full epitaph appears in Osborn:
Here lies thrown, for the Worms to eat,
Little Bossive Robin, that was so great.
Not Robin-Goodfellow, nor Robin Hood,
But Robin the Encloser of Hatfield Wood.
Who seem'd as sent from ugly Fate,
To spoil the Prince and rob the State.

Owning a Mind of dismal ends,
As Traps for Foes, and Tricks for Friends.
But now in Hatfield *lies the* ——
Who stank while he liv'd, and died of the —. (Osborn, 412-13).

[55] [Hay's note: Coming to an Inn, where he was expected, before his Attendants, the Mistress of the House, seeing a plain Person, of very mean Aspect, ordered him to assist in getting things ready for Philopœmen. His Attendants finding him so employed, he told them, he was then paying the Tribute of his Ugliness. *Plutarch*;] A legendary Achaean general, Philopœmen (d. 183 B.C.) was noted for "the meanness of his Habit, the homeliness of his Garb, and the easy plainness of his Conversation" (*Plutarch's Lives in Eight Volumes*, vol. 3 [London, 1749], 270).

[56] [Hay's note: In his Essay on Physiognomy.] This passage appears in the Cotton translation: "That superficial Ugliness, which nevertheless is always the most imperious, is of least Prejudice to the State of the Mind, and of little Certainty in the Opinion of Men. The other, which by a more proper Name, is call'd a more substantial Deformity, strikes deeper in" (*Essays of Michael Seigneur de Montaigne*, trans. Charles Cotton, vol. 3 [London, 1700], 453). In contrast to Hay's argument, Montaigne asserts earlier, "There is nothing more likely than a Conformity and Relation of the Body to the Soul" (453).

[57] emended from "at"

[58] [Hay's note: Edicto vetuit, ne quis se præter Apellen
Pingeret, aut alius Lysippo ducerat æra
Fortis Alexandri voltum simulantia.—*Hor. Ep.* I. L. 2. See too Cicero's celebrated Epistle to Lucceius.] Trans: "[B]y an edict [he] forbade anyone save Apelles to paint him, or any other than Lysippus to model bronze in copying the features of brave Alexander" (Horace, "Book 2, Epistle 1," *Satires, Epistles and Ars Poetica*, trans. H. Rushton Fairclough [Cambridge, MA: Harvard University Press, 1920], 417).

[59] [Hay's note: From the Translation, and Notes, of the Epistle I have mentioned.] Hay cites William Melmoth's translation of Cicero's letter to Lucius Lucceius along with Melmoth's note to the letter without marking the difference between the two. Melmoth's note begins with the discussion of Agesilaus as "one of the most considerable persons of his age" and continues to the end of the quotation (Marcus Tullius Cicero, *The Letters of Marcus Tullius Cicero to Several of his Friends*, vol. 1, trans. William Melmoth [London: R. Dodsley, 1753], 83-4).

[60] [Hay's note: Si curatus inæquali tonsore capillos
Occurri, rides; si forte subucula pexæ
Trita subest tunicæ, vel si toga dissidet impar,
Rides: quid, mea cum pugnat sententia secum ?
Quod petiit, spernit ; repetit quod nuper omisit ?
Æstuat, et vitæ disconvenit ordine toto ?
Diruit, ædificat, mutat quadrata rotundis ?
Insanire putas solemnia me; neque rides.]
Trans: Maecenas, you notice and laugh if the barber gives me
A crooked haircut or if my worn-out shirt
Shows under the new tunic I just bought
Or if my toga doesn't hang down straight.
But when I don't know what my own mind is,

Hating the thing I just now loved, and wanting
The thing I just rejected scornfully,
Judgment seething and boiling, the order of things
All out of order, pulled down, built up again,
Pulled down, built up, round turned to square, and square
To round again, you're perfectly unperturbed
And not the least disposed to laugh at me.
("Epistle 1," *The Epistles of Horace*, trans. David Ferry, 11).

[61] [Hay's note: The 7th of the 15th Book in the Translation—the 32d of the 10th in the Original.] In Melmoth's translation, Asinius Pollio's account of Balbus' excesses concludes with the story of "a certain noted auctioneer in the city of Hispalis" who was exposed to wild beasts "for no other reason but because the poor man was excessively deformed. Such is the monster with whom I had the misfortune to be connected!" (352).

[62] Hay jumbles the order and excises a Latin tag from Bacon's essay. The passage in the original reads, "Certainly there is a consent between the body and the mind, and where Nature erreth in the one, she ventureth in the other; *Ubi peccat in uno, periclitatur in altero.* But because there is in Man an Election touching the Frame of his mind, and a Necessity in the Frame of his body, the Stars of natural Inclination are sometimes obscured by the Sun of Discipline and Vertue: Therefore it is good to consider of *Deformity*, not as a Sign which is more deceiveable, but as a Cause which seldome faileth of the Effect" (Francis Bacon, *Essayes and Counsels, Civil and Moral* [London, 1664], 246.)

[63] Bacon appears to have misapplied 2 Timothy 3.2-3 in which Paul prophesies the depth of human evil, not just that of the deformed, preceding the apocalypse: "For men shall be lovers of their own selves, covetous, boasters, proud, blasphemers, disobedient to parents, unthankful, unholy,/Without natural affection, trucebreakers, false accusers, incontinent, fierce, despisers of those that are good" (KJV). A similar list also appears in Romans 1:31.

[64] [Hay's note: Juv. Sat. 13.] In context the passage reads, "casus multis hic cognitus ac iam/tritus et e medio fortunae ductus acervo" (lines 9-10). Trans: "Such a mishap has been known to many; it is one of the common kind, plucked at random out of Fortune's heap" (*Juvenal and Persius*, trans. G.G. Ramsay [London: William Heinemann, 1920], 247). Montaigne cites the same passage in his essay "Of Glory" (*Essays of Michael, Seigneur de Montaigne*, trans. Charles Cotton, vol. 2. [London, 1700], 486).

[65] The founder of Greek atomic theory, Democritus (460-357? B.C.), perhaps on the strength of his On Cheerfulness was misrepresented by Latin writers as "the laughing philosopher" (*Oxford Companion to Classical Literature*).

[66] Executed for their adherence to Protestantism during Mary I's (1516-1558, acc. 1553) reconciliation with Rome, Thomas Cranmer (1489-1556), Hugh Latimer (1485-1555), and Nicholas Ridley (c. 1503-1555) are collectively known as the Oxford Martyrs for their place of execution.

[67] [Hay's note: Donec labantes consilio patres
        Firmaret auctor nunquam aliàs dato,
            Interque mœrentes amicos
                Egregius properaret exul.

58

Atqui sciebat quæ sibi barbarus
Tortor pararet: —————— tamen
Dimovit obstantes propinquos,
Et populum reditus morantem.
                    Hor. Od. 5. l. 3.]
Trans.: "Till he should strengthen the Senate's wavering purpose by advice ne'er
given before, and amid sorrowing friends should hurry forth a glorious exile. Full
well he knew what the barbarian torturer was making ready for him; and yet he
pushed aside the kinsmen who blocked his path and the people who would stay
his going" (Horace, *The Odes and Epodes*, trans. C.E. Bennet [Cambridge: Harvard
University Press, 1968], 199). This ode to martial courage celebrates the Roman
general Marcus Atilius Regulus (d. ca 250 B.C.) who, as a captive of the Carthag-
inians, was sent to negotiate peace with Rome in 255 B.C. Advising the Romans
to continue the war, he returned to prison in Carthage where he died. The story
of his death by torture made him a national hero (*Oxford Companion to Classical
Literature*).

[68] [Hay's note: En vain ses Ministres & les plus considérables Seigneurs du Royaume
firent tous leurs efforts, pour le faire changer de résolution. Il répondit à tout
ce qu'on lui disoit là-dessus, que quand la bonne foy seroit bannie du reste du
monde, il falloit qu'on la trouvât toûjours dans la bouche des Rois. Histoire de
France, par le P. G. Daniel.] This is attributed by le Père Gabriel Daniel (1649-
1728) to John II "The Good" (1319-1364) (*Histoire de France Depuis L'établissement
de la monarchie françoise dans les Gaules*,vol. 3 [Paris, 1722], 714). Defeated at
Poitiers in 1356, John II was imprisoned in England until 1360 when under the
terms of the Treaty of Brétigny his son, Louis of Anjou, took his place. Upon
Louis' escape and, therefore, breach of parole, John II returned willingly to Eng-
land in 1364, dying a few months later (John Bell Henneman, Jr., "John II the
Good," *Medieval France: An Encyclopedia*, ed. William W. Kibler and Gover A. Zinn
[New York: Garland, 1995]).

[69] [Hay's note: Recordatus quondam super cœnam, quod nihil cuiquam toto die
præstitisset, memorabilem illam meritoque laudatam vocem edidit : AMICI,
DIEM PERDIDI.—Suetonius.] Trans: "[R]emembering at dinner that he had
done nothing for anybody all that day, he gave utterance to that memorable and
praiseworthy remark: 'Friends, I have lost a day'" (Suetonius, "Titus," *The Lives of
the Caesars*, vol. 2., trans. J. C. Rolfe [London: William Heinemann, 1920], 331).

[70] [Hay's note: Echard's Roman History.] Hadrian's "Moderation and Clemency
appear'd by his pardoning the Injuries that were done him before he was Emperor; and having once met a Person who had offended him, he said, *You have
escaped, since I am made Emperor*" (Laurence Echard, *The Roman history from the settle-
ment of the empire by Augustus Caesar to the removal of the imperial seat by Constantine
the Great* [London, 1698], 307). Publius Aelius Hadrianus (A.D. 76–138) was
Roman emperor (A.D. 117–138).

[71] [Hay's note: Mezerai, & Daniel.] Louis XII (1462-1515, reigned 1498-1515). See
François Eudes de Mezeray, *A General Chronological History of France*, trans. John
Bulteel (London, 1683) and Daniel, *Histoire de France*.

[72] Jonas Hanway, *An Historical Account of the British Trade over the Caspian Sea*, vol. 2
(London, 1753), 141-150.

[73] Henry IV (1553-1610).

[74] See Maximilien de Béthune, duc de Sully, *Mémoires, ou, Oeconomies Royales d'Etat, Domestiques, Politiques et Militaires de Henri le Grand*, 12 vols. (Amsterdam, 1725).

[75] [Hay's note: Moreri's Dictionary.—Turkish Spy. Vol. I. B. 2. Let. 20.] "Above 50 Historians, and 500 Panegyrists, Poets and Orators have spoken of this Prince with Praise" (Louis Moréri and Edmund Bohun, *The Great Historical, Geographical and Poetical Dictionary being a Curious Miscellany of Sacred and Prophane History* [London, 1694]). See also Giovanni Palo Marana, *The Eight Volumes of Letters Writ by a Turkish Spy who Lived Five and Forty Years Undiscover'd, at Paris*, trans. Daniel Saltmarsh, vol. 1 (London, 1694) 164-76.

[76] Louis XIV (1638-1715).

[77] According to his nephew and biographer, Francis Tutté, Hay was involved in 1743 in the experimental manufacture of silk in Spitalfields, London (*The Works of William Hay, esq.* [London, 1794], vii).

[78] The legendary Procrustes made travellers fit his bed by stretching the short or amputating the limbs of the tall. Phalaris (570-554 B.C.), tryant of Agrigentum in Sicily, burned his victims alive in a bronze bull. Their cries were supposed to resemble a bull's bellowing.

[79] Broughton opened his boxing theatre in 1742 in Hanway Street, Oxford Street in London. (DNB)

[80] emended from "Assembles."

[81] The passage in Bacon reads, "Kings in ancient Times (and at this present in some Countreys) were wont to put great Trust in *Eunuchs*; because they that are envious towards all, are more obnoxious and officious toward one. But yet their Trust towards them hath rather been as to good Spials, and good Whisperers, then good Magistrates and Officers" (Bacon, *Essayes and Counsels* [1664], 247).

[82] [Hay's note: Sat. 10.] Satire 10, Line 356.

[83] [Hay's note: Hor. Ep. 2. l. 2.] Book 2, Epistle 2 (to Julius Florus), Line 211.

[84] See *Spectator* 17: "It is happy for a Man, that has any of these Oddnesses about him, if he can be as merry upon himself as others are apt to be upon that Occasion."

[85] White's chocolate-house was associated with gambling. In his essay "On Modern Education" Jonathan Swift writes, "I have heard, that the late Earl of *Oxford*, in the time of his Ministry, never passed by White's Chocolate-House (the common Rendezvous of infamous Sharpers and noble Cullies) without bestowing a Curse upon that famous Academy, as the Bane of half the *English* Nobility" (*The Intelligencer* [Dublin: A. Moor, 1729], 88).

[86] It was the custom for the court to appear in their finest on the monarch's birthday.

[87] emended from "invates."

[88] Abraham Cowley, "The Waiting Maid" lines 13-16.

[89] [Hay's note: Formam optat modico pueris, majore puellis
                    Murmure cum Veneris fanum videt anxia mater,
                    Usque ad delicias votorum.—Sat. 10.] Trans.: "When the loving mother passes the temple of Venus, she prays in whispered breath for her boys—more loudly, and entering into the most trifling particulars, for her daughers—that they may have beauty" (lines 289-291) (Juvenal, "Satire 10," *Juve-*

60

nal and Persius, trans. G.G. Ramsay [London: William Heniemann, 1920] 215).

90 [Hay's note: *Sacharissa* belongs to *Waller, Myra* to *Landsdown, Cloe* to *Prior,* and *Belinda* to Pope.] Edmund Waller (1606-1687); George Granville, Baron Lansdowne (1667-1735); Matthew Prior (1664-1721). The pseudonymous female characters are not alike. Sacharissa, for example, was Waller's poetic name for Lady Dorothy Sidney whom he courted in vain through poetry until her marriage in 1639. Belinda, however, was Pope's name for Arabella Fermor, the subject of *The Rape of the Lock.*

91 [Hay's note: Milton Par. Lost. b. 8] "Not words alone pleased her" (8.57). Eve prefers Adam over Raphael as storyteller because she knows that, unlike the archangel, Adam will "intermix/Grateful digressions, and solve high dispute/With conjugal caresses" (8.54-56).

92 [Hay's note: In his Poem on Love.] "While her high pride does scarce descend/ To mark their follies" (lines 34-35) (Edmund Waller, "Of Love," *Poems,* ed. G. Thorn Drury [New York: Greenwood Press, 1968] 88).

93 [Hay's note: *Merry Wives of Windsor.*]

94 [Hay's note: Sed vetat optari faciem Lucretia, qualem
                      Ipsa habuit. Cuperet RutilæVirginia gibbum
                      Accipere, atque suum Rutilæ dare.—Sat. 10.] Trans.: "[B]ut Lurcetia forbids us to pray for a face like her own/ and Virginia would gladly take Rutila's hump and give her own fair form to Rutila" (lines 293-95) (Juvenal, "Satire 10," *Juvenal and Persius*, trans. Ramsay, 215).

95 [Hay's note: —Nullus ephebum
                      Deformem, sæva castravit in arce tyrannus.
                      Nec prætextatum rapuit Nero loripedem, nec
                      Strumosum, atque utero pariter gibboque tumentem. *ibid.*] Trans.: "No misshapen youth was ever unsexed by cruel tyrant in his castle; never did Nero seize a bandy-legged or scrofulous favourite, or one that was humpbacked or pot-bellied!" (lines 306-09) (Juvenal, "Satire 10," *Juvenal and Persius*, trans. Ramsay, 217).

96 [Hay's note: Hic se præcipitem tecto dedit: ille flagellis
                      Ad mortem cæsus: fugiens hic decidit acrem
                      Prædonum in turbam: dedit hic pro corpore nummos:
                      Hunc preminxerunt calones: quin etiam illud
                      Accidit, ut cuidam testes caudamque falacem
                      Demeteret ferrum.—Hor. Sat. 2. 1. I.] Trans.: "One man has thrown himself headlong from the roof; another has been flogged to death; a third, in his flight, has fallen into a savage gang of robbers; another has paid a price to save his life; another been abused [ie. urinated upon] by stable-boys; nay, once it so befell that a man cut off with the sword the testicles and lustful member" (lines 41-46) (Horace, "Book 1, Satire 2," *Satires, Epistles and Ars Poetica,* trans. H. Rushton Fairclough [Cambridge, MA: Harvard University Press, 1920] 21, 23).

Hay's note: —Quosdam mœchos & mugilis intrat. Juv. ib.] Trans.: "Some adulterers undergo the punishment of the mullet" (line 317) (Juvenal, "Satire 10," *Juvenal and Persius*, trans. Ramsay, 217).

[97] [Hay's note: —Optimus hic & formosissimus idem
Gentis Patriciæ rapitur miser extinguendus
Messalinæ oculis. —Juv. Sat. 10.] Trans : "Best and fairest of a patrician house, the unhappy youth is dragged to destruction by Messalina's eyes" (lines 331-333) (Juvenal, "Satire 10," *Juvenal and Persius*, trans. Ramsay, 217, 219).

[98] [Hay's note: Suetonius.] In Book 6 of *The Lives of the Caesars* Suetonius records that Nero "castrated the boy Sporus and actually tried to make a woman of him; and he married him with all the usual ceremonies, including a dowry and a bridal veil, took him to his house attended by a great throng, and treated him as his wife" (trans. J.C. Rolfe, vol. 2 [London: William Heinemann, 1920], 130-131).

[99] [Hay's note: Hunc optent generum Rex & Regina: puellæ
Hunc rapiant: quidquid calcaverit hic, rosa fiat.
Ast ego nutrici non mando vota; negato
Jupiter hæc illi.—Pers. Sat. 2.] Like Juvenal's tenth satire, this one rails against foolish prayers. At lines 37-38, Persius puts into the mouth of an elderly female a prayer for an infant and then rejects the petition: "'May kings and queens desire him for their daughter! May the maidens scramble for him! May roses bloom wherever he plants his foot!' No! never shall prayer of mine be committed to a nurse; reject, O Jupiter, her petition" (Persius, "Satire 2," *Juvenal and Persius*, trans. Ramsay, 339).

[100] [Hay's note: Gen. c. 39.] Genesis 39 recounts the story of Joseph's rejection of Potiphar's wife and Joseph's subsequent imprisonment.

[101] [Hay's note: —Quid prosuit olim
Hippolyto grave propositum? Quid Bellerophonti?
Erubuit nempe hæc, ceu fastidita repulsa :
Nec Sthenobœa minus quam Cressa excanduit, & se
Concusere ambæ. —Juv. Sat. 10.] "[W]hat availed Hippolytus or Bellerophon their firm resolve? The Cretan lady (Phaedra) flared up as though repelled with scorn; no less furious was Sthenoboea. Both spurred themselves to fury" (lines 324-328) (Juvenal, "Satire 10," *Juvenal and Persius*, trans. Ramsay, 217).

[Hay's note: Ut Prœtum mulier perfida credulum
Falsis impulerit criminibus, nimis
Casto Bellerophontae
Maturare necem, refert.
Narrat pæne datum Pelea Tartaro,
Magnessam Hippolyten dum fugit abstinens.
Hor. Od. 7. 1. 3.] "She tells how a perfidious woman by false charges drove credulous Proetus to bring swift death on over-chaste Bellerophon. She tells of Peleus, all but doomed to Tartarus for righteous shunning of Magnessian Hippolyte" (lines 13-19) (Horace, "Book 3, Ode 7," *The Odes and Epodes*, trans. C.E. Bennet [London: William Heinemann, 1968], 205).

[102] "The Motto" (lines 1-2) (Abraham Cowley, *Poems*, ed. A.R. Waller [Cambridge: Cambridge University Press, 1905], 15).

[103] [Hay's note: Quid te exempta juvat spinis de pluribus una?
Hor. Ep. 2. 1. 2] Trans. : "What have you gained if you've plucked out just one

62

thorn out of many?"(line 212)(Horace, "Epistle 2, Book 2," trans. Ferry, 149). The cleansing of the Augean stables and the slaying of Cacus and Hydra were three of Hercules' labours.

[104] Edward Hyde, Earl of Clarendon (1609-1674) recounts Sir Charles Cavendish's (1591-1654) service in spite of his deformity in the civil war alongside his brother, the Marquis of Newcastle. See *The History of the Rebellion and Civil Wars in England*, vol. 2 (Oxford, 1703), 389.

[105] Theophilus Cibber records that Samuel Garth (1661-1719), physician and poet, was buried alongside his wife "in the church of Harrow on the Hill . . . in a vault he caused to be built for himself and his family" (*The Lives Of the Poets of Great Britain and Ireland*, vol. 3 [London, 1753], 272).

[106] [Hay's note: Juv. Sat. 10.] Trans.: "seeing that even sepulchres have their doom assigned to them" (line 146) (Juvenal, "Satire 10," *Juvenal and Persius*, trans. Ramsay, 205).

[107] [Hay's note: Spectator, No 169.] Cyrus "pleased, that while his Soul returned to him who made it, his Body should incorporate with the great Mother of all things, and by that means become beneficial to Mankind. For which Reason, he gives his sons a positive Order not to enshrine it in Gold or Silver, but to lay it in the Earth as soon as the life was gone out of it" (*Spectator* 169).

[108] [Hay's note: I will here give a more particular Account of my self with regard to that Distemper, which I hope will be of more immediate Service.]

[109] The founder of the present-day British Museum.

[110] In March of 1740, Parliament paid Joanna Stephens the exceptional sum of £5,000 for her recipe to cure the stone. Prior to the payment, Parliamentary trustees appointed to investigate her claims included such colleagues of William Hay as Arthur Onslow and Robert Walpole. Comprising a powder, a decoction, and pills, the medicine underwent several trials by physicians in Britain and France to discover its lithontriptic properties. By taking either the solid form of Mrs. Stephens's medicine, castile soap, or lime-water, Hay ingested the lime that Stephen Hales concluded in his experiments was the agent that broke up but did not completely dissolve bladder stones. By publishing his case, Hay contributes to a lively eighteenth-century debate on lithontriptics while also defending his government's purchase of the recipe. See Arthur J. Viseltear, "Joanna Stephens and the Eighteenth-Century Lithontriptics; A Misplaced Chapter in the History of Therapeutics," *Bulletin of the History of Medicine* 42 (1968): 199-220. Contemporary discussion includes David Hartley, *Ten Cases of Persons who have taken Mrs. Stephens's Medicines for the Stone* (London, 1738); James Kirkpatrick, *An Account of the Success of Mrs. Stephens's Medicines for the Stone* (Belfast, 1739); Joanna Stephens, *A Most Excellent Cure for the Stone and Gravel* (London, 1740?); Stephen Hales, *An Account of Some Experiments and Observations on Mrs. Stephens's Medicines for Dissolving the Stone* (London, 1740); Richard Gem, *An Account of the Remedy for the Stone, Lately Published in England* (London, 1741); James Parsons, *A Description of the Human Urinary Bladder, and Parts Belonging to it* (London, 1742); John Rutty, *A Particular Account of Mrs. Stephens's Method of Preparing and Giving the Medicine for the Stone and Gravel* (London, 1750).

[111] See William Hogarth, *The Analysis of Beauty. Written with a view of fixing the fluctuating ideas of taste* (London, 1753).

[112] Page 10 in this copy.

* [Hay's note: N.B. Many Ladies say, that Shock is as ugly a Cur as myself, and un-
worthy of his Post. But nothing so disrespectful shall ever escape me; lest it would
offend, or be thought the Envy of a Rival.]